MRS BEETON SAYS...

A new musical based on the life
and times of Isabella Beeton

Book by Helen Watts

Music and lyrics by Eamonn O'Dwyer

ISBN 978-0-573-11664-3

www.concordtheatricals.co.uk

www.concordtheatricals.com

For Amateur Production Enquiries

United Kingdom and World
excluding North America

licensing@concordtheatricals.co.uk

020-7054-7200

Each title is subject to availability from Concord Theatricals, depending upon country of performance.

MUSIC USE NOTE

MRS BEETON SAYS...

First performed at the Redgrave Theatre, Bristol, 6 December 2018, by Bristol Old Vic Theatre School

ISABELLA BEETON	Beshlie Thorp
SAM BEETON	Jonathan Oldfield
ALICE	Heidi Parsons
SARAH	Anna-Kate Golding
AMABEL	Karla Kaucky
MYRA BROWNE	Eva O'Hara
COMMENTATOR/CORSET MAN/DOCTOR	Shane David-Joseph
FRED GREENWOOD/BARKER	Lawrence Haynes

Other parts played by members of the company

Piano	Pamela Rudge
Violin	Wendhy Sierra
Cello	Christine Johnstone

Director	Paul Clarkson
Musical Director	Pamela Rudge
Designer	Bronia Housman
Choreographer	Clare Fox
Lighting Designer	Joe Stathers
Sound Designer	Evie Nichols
Voice Coach	Carol Fairlamb
Dialect Coach	James Gitsham
Assistant Director	Sara Malik

Production Manager	Jon Sherwood
Production SM Supervisor	Alix Abram
Stage Manager	Eve Kershaw
Deputy Stage Manager	James Goldsworthy
Assistant Stage Managers	Rosie Tredray, Charlotte Woolley
Production Electrician	Chris Horseman
Lighting Operator	Jack Tosney
Sound Operator	Daniel Davies
Prop Maker	Hebe Perry
Construction Manager	Andy Scrivens

Set Construction	Maya Barker, Daniel Davies, Ambra Fuller, Harriet Hollinshead-Lee, Jack Tosney, Rosie Tredray, Oliver Wareham, Charlotte Woolley
Scenic Art	Julie O'Conner, Emma Inge, Radhika Parekh, Daisy Tomlin
Costume Supervisor	Janie Powell
Costume Assistants	Amber Bowerman, Isabel Cope, Madi Barnicoat

Mrs Beeton Says... was originally commissioned by Bristol Old Vic Theatre School in 2018.

MRS BEETON SAYS... SONG LIST

1: Mrs Beeton Says...	Women
1b: Before Epsom	Underscore
2: Epsom	Commentator and Company
3: Transition	Women
3a: Together	Undersore
4: I Love A List	Bella
5: I Belong To You	Bella and Sam
6a: Letter – On Fabric	Fabric Woman
6b: Letter – On Entertaining	Entertainment Woman
6c: Letter – On Corsetry	Corset Man
6d: Letter – From Cupid's Letter Bag	Cupid's Letter Bag Woman
6e: Fred	Underscore
7: You There	Bella, Sarah and Amabel
8: How We Rise	Barker and Company
9: Samuel – 25th August 1857	Women
10: Give A Girl A Book	Bella, Sam and Women
10b: Into The Streets	Underscore
10c: She Knew Your Name	Underscore
11: Wisdom	Women
11b: Bella Reads	Underscore
12: All Things To All Men	Bella and Women
13: Kitchen Trials	Bella
14: You There (Reprise)	Bella
15: Office. 1860	Underscore
16: The Grand Tour	Company
17: Watch The Light	Bella
18: Reviews	Company
18b: Transition into Butcher's	Underscore
18c: Transition into Bella's Kitchen	Underscore
19: Don't You See	Myra and Bella
20: Trial, 1865	Underscore
21: Usque Ad Finem	Underscore
22: Finale – The Domestic Anthem	Women

AUTHOR'S NOTE ON CASTING

Other characters, spoken letters and voice-overs may be distributed among the company at the discretion of the Director. In the original production the actors playing Bella and Sam did not play any other roles, but the remaining four women and two men multi-roled all the other ensemble parts. Accents should represent the full variety and breadth of the British Isles.

SETTING

The action of the play takes place predominantly in London.

TIME

1854–1865.

CHARACTERS

Cast size optional – min 5F 3M

ISABELLA (BELLA) BEETON – (f, 20s) A bright and ambitious
young (woman
SAM BEETON – (m, 20–30s) Her husband, an
entrepreneurial publisher
BESSIE – Isabella's sister (20)
ESTHER – Isabella's sister (18)
COMMENTATOR – (m, any age)

MYRA BROWNE – (f, 20s) A middle-class Clapham housewife
ALICE – (f, 18) A West Country maid
SARAH – (f, 20–40s) A Northern mother of eight
AMABEL – (f, 20–40s) A wealthy London society lady

FRED GREENWOOD – (m, 20–30s) Sam Beeton's assistant
FABRIC WOMAN – (f, 30–60s)
ENTERTAINING WOMAN – (f, 20–30s)
CORSET MAN – (m, any age)
CUPID'S LETTER BAG WOMAN – (f, 20–40s)

BARKER – (m, 20s–60s) A side-show performer & social
commentator
PETE JONES/CHARLIE BROWNE/LORD CADOGAN – (m, 20–40s)
PEGGY JONES – (f, any age)
SALLY VINE – (f, 20s)

GEORGE FREEMAN – (m 30–50s) A chauvinistic engraver
PROSTITUTE – (f, any age)

CALF'S FEET WOMAN – (f, any age)
TRIPE WOMAN – (f, any age)
SNIPES WOMAN – (f, any age)
HORSERADISH SAUCE WOMAN – (f, any age)
RABBIT STEW MAN – (m, any age)
SYLLABUB WOMAN – (f, any age)

ENGLISH TOURISTS – (any ages)
FRENCH SHOP ASSISTANT – (f, any age)
GERMAN WOMAN – (f, any age)
DOCTOR – (m, any age)
BUTCHER – (m, any age)
JUDGE – (m, 30–60's)

[MUSIC NO. 1. "MRS BEETON SAYS..."]

We see four WOMEN, *in four separate kitchens, reading from* Mrs Beeton's Book of Household Management. *They read aloud from the book in turn.*

MYRA
MRS BEETON SAYS ...

ALICE "As with the commander of an army, or the leader of any enterprise, so is it with the mistress of a house"

SARAH
MRS BEETON SAYS ...

AMABEL "To be a good housewife does not necessarily imply the abandonment of proper pleasures"

ALICE
MRS BEETON SAYS ...

MYRA "The mistress of the house is the first and the last, the Alpha and the Omega in the government of her establishment"

AMABEL
MRS BEETON SAYS...

SARAH "She is a person of far more importance in a community than she usually thinks she is"

MYRA
MRS BEETON SAYS THE THINGS A WOMAN NEEDS TO KNOW

SARAH
HOW TO RUN YOUR HOUSEHOLD,

AMABEL
RAISE YOUR CHILDREN,

MYRA
ROAST YOUR CHICKEN,

ALICE
KNEAD YOUR DOUGH!

AMABEL
MRS BEETON SAYS HER METHODS SET A GIRL APART,

ALL
MRS BEETON SAYS TO BE A WOMAN TAKES A CERTAIN KIND OF ART.

MYRA "Man is a *dining* animal. Creatures of the inferior races eat and drink; man only *dines*."

SARAH and **ALICE**
MRS BEETON KNOWS HOW SUET PUDDING SHOULD BE MADE.

MYRA and **AMABEL**
MRS BEETON TELLS US WHAT TO SERVE AT LUNCH,

AMABEL
HOW TABLES SHOULD BE LAID.

ALL
MRS BEETON MAKES IT ALL SO SIMPLE AND CONCISE;
MRS BEETON KNOWS THAT EVERY WOMAN NEEDS A WOMAN'S GOOD ADVICE.

SARAH "There is no more fruitful source of family discontent than badly cooked dinners and untidy ways..."

ALL
TIME WAS ...
YOU WERE EXPECTED TO JUST KNOW THE THINGS THAT NO ONE EVER TOLD YOU.
TIME WAS...
YOU BURNT THE BISCUITS,
WOKE THE BABY
TORE THE LINEN
AND YOUR HOUSEMAID
OR YOUR HUSBAND

OR YOUR MOTHER
OR HIS MOTHER
WOULD THINK LESS OF YOU,
IMPRESS ON YOU
THE NEED FOR YOU
TO TRY AND DO
A BETTER JOB OF DOING ALL THE THINGS THAT NO ONE EVER
 SHOWED YOU HOW...
BUT NOW...

MRS BEETON TEACHES US THE RUDIMENTS OF LIFE;
HOW TO BE A LADY AND A MOTHER AND A HOSTESS AND A
 WIFE.
MRS BEETON SHARES WITH US HER WISDOM AND HER GRACE
MRS BEETON KNOWS THAT EVERY WOMAN HAS A
 BATTLEFIELD TO FACE.

MRS BEETON LIKENS US TO GEN'RALS OFF TO WAR!
MRS BEETON KNOWS EACH DAY IS HARDER THAN THE DAY
 THAT WENT BEFORE.
MRS BEETON TELLS US WE ARE SISTERS IN THIS FIGHT.
WHETHER IT'S THE DINNER
OR THE CHILDREN
OR THE WEANING
OR THE FLOWERS
OR THE MEASLES
OR THE LINEN
OR THE CLEANING
JUST KNOWING THERE'S AN ANSWER AND A METHOD AND A
 MEANING
GIVES ME HOPE THAT I AM DOING SOMETHING RIGHT ...
MOTHERS, SISTERS, DAUGHTERS, WIVES,

MRS BEETON SAYS...UNITE!

MYRA   (*reading from* Mrs Beeton's Book of Household
Management) "If I had known that this book would have
cost me the labour which it has, I should never have been
courageous enough to commence it."

The song ends, and MYRA *is left on the stage.*

(showing the huge book to the audience) "Mrs Beeton's Book of Household Management". Just look at the size of it!

I imagined Mrs Beeton to be stout, red-faced, covered in flour and dripping. There was *no* question in my mind that she wasn't a formidable middle-aged matron with decades of culinary experience. I mean... *(referring to the book)* Look at it! Her household must be a kingdom of organisation!! –"a place for everything and everything in its place."

Before I got married, I used to imagine what it would be like to be the mistress of a house. I imagined my devoted husband sitting by the fire with two or three little darlings playing with their toys; a maid would keep away the dust, a housekeeper would keep everything in order and, of course, a cook would prepare delicious dinners! That was the dream, and then I married Charlie – an insurance man from Putney...so that was the end of that. I would have to be the maid, housekeeper and cook. I had never so much as boiled an egg or ironed a shirt, but how hard could it be?!

[MUSIC NO. 1b. "BEFORE EPSOM"]

1854 31st May.

The company are at the races and watching with binoculars.

ISABELLA *(eighteen) has recently returned home from her school in Germany.* **ISABELLA** *is dodging through the crowds during the race with her two sisters* **ESTHER** *and* **BESSIE**. *All three girls have estuary accents that lean to cockney when excited.* **SAM** *(twenty three) has had an unlucky day gambling on the horses.*

BELLA   Bessie! Esther! Get over here!

BESSIE   Can you see the finish line?

BELLA   Yes! *(squeezing past people)* 'scuse me sir... *(calling)* Hurry, the race is about to start!

BESSIE   Where's Mama?

BELLA She's taken all the children for a walk with Granny.

BESSIE It must seem strange for some of the younger ones to see their home over-run with people.

BELLA The grandstand is hardly a home, more somewhere we all sleep when there isn't a race.

BESSIE Still, they don't know any better.

ESTHER spots SAM as she scrambles past him. She hurries to gossip with her sisters.

ESTHER Did you see who we just passed?

BESSIE No –

BELLA Who?

ESTHER That's Sam Beeton.

[MUSIC NO. 2. "EPSOM"]

BELLA *(in disbelief)* No! *(She stands on tiptoe to get a look at him/looks through binoculars?)*

BESSIE Who's he? I mean I know the name –

ESTHER You know Eliza and Viccie's older brother.

BESSIE The one who went to prison?

ESTHER No, the other one! The publisher, Samuel Orchart Beeton. You know! Owns a huge publishing house on the Strand...

BESSIE *(clearly disappointed)* Oh!! I thought he was meant to be good-looking?

ESTHER He's not *bad*-looking... *(asking her opinion)* Bella, what do you think?

BELLA I think he's delicious!

The girls squeal with delight.

COMMENTATOR
LOVELY WARM, SUNNY DAY HERE FOR THE EPSOM DERBY
THE HORSES ARE LOOKING BRIGHT-EYED AND READY TO
   GO ... OH!
HOSPODAR'S LOOKING A BIT FRISKY ON THE OUTSIDE,
HE'LL NEED TO SIMMER DOWN A BIT BEFORE THEY BEGIN.
THERE'S LORD DERVISH IN THE MIDDLE OF THE FIELD AT
   FIVE TO ONE
BEING THE HOT FAVOURITE TO WIN.
ANDOVER SEVEN TO TWO, KING TOM TEN TO ONE, HOSPODAR
   ELEVEN TO ONE,
HERMIT THIRTY-THREE TO ONE, OH... THEY'RE BEING CALLED
   TO LINE UP!
ANDOVER AND KING TOM LOOKING *VERY* FINE INDEED ...

BELLA Mr Beeton?

   SAM *looks up at her.*

SAM Yes?

BELLA *(coyly)* You don't remember me, do you? We used to
play together as children... (**SAM** *looks perplexed*) ...when
you used to visit your grandmother in Milk Street.

SAM *(remembering)* Isabella Mayson?! You're so grown up!
My sisters sometimes talk about you in their letters from
Germany. Will you be seeing them soon?

BELLA I doubt it. I've left school now.

BESSIE Bella! Quick, the race is about to start!

COMMENTATOR
THERE'S THE SIGNAL AND THEY'RE *OFF*!
TWENTY-SEVEN HORSES HAVE MADE A BEAUTIFUL START,
HOSPODAR IS TAKING AN EARLY LEAD,
WITH MARC ANTONY, CANUTE, AND WILD HUNTSMAN
   FOLLOWING BEHIND;
ANDOVER GATHERING FULL STRIDE, DERVISH, KING TOM,
AND SETTLING TOWARDS THE BACK MARSYAS, NEW WARRIOR,
AND THE EARLY BIRD BRINGING UP THE REAR.

NOW THEY'RE APPROACHING ABOUT HALF WAY,
HOSPODAR IS BEING PURSUED BY ANDOVER, WITH
MARC ANTONY AND KING TOM DROPPING OFF –

There are frenzied shouts from the crowd as the race comes to its end.

SAM Come on King Tom!

BELLA Come on Andover!

There is a rivalry between them.

CHORUS
AAAAH!

COMMENTATOR
WHAT'S THIS? HERMIT HAS NOW TAKEN THE LEAD,
WITH ANDOVER CLOSE BEHIND,
KING TOM, DERVISH, KNIGHT OF ST GEORGE, MARSYAS,
EARLY BIRD, AND NEW WARRIOR!
KING TOM DESP'RATELY TRYING TO GET AHEAD,
BUT IT'S NO GOOD! KING TOM CAN'T GO ON!

SAM Come on!!!

BELLA Looks like you backed the wrong horse Mr. Beeton!

COMMENTATOR
HE DOESN'T HAVE THE PACE!
THE TWO LEADERS ARE BEGINNING TO WEAKEN

ALL
SENDING ANDOVER INTO THE LEAD!

COMMENTATOR
KING TOM IS DESP'RATELY TRYING TO MOVE FORWARD BUT
IT'S NO GOOD!
ANDOVER! ANDOVER!
ANDOVER STRIDES AHEAD AND WINS THE DERBY!

The crowd celebrate the win.

SAM (*frustrated at losing*) Bugger!

SAM *tears up his losing ticket.*

BELLA I'd best collect my winnings. Goodbye Mr. Beeton.

SAM Will I see you again?

BELLA *(coyly)* Perhaps… If you need any tips.

She leaves.

[MUSIC NO. 3. "TRANSITION"]

CHORUS *(variously)*

MRS BEETON SAYS…

"Friendships should not be hastily formed, nor the heart given at once to every newcomer."

MRS BEETON SAYS…

"Care must be taken that the love of company, for its own sake, does not become a prevailing passion."

MRS BEETON SAYS…

"There *are* ladies who uniformly smile at everything, and who do not possess the courage to reprehend vice."

MRS BEETON SAYS…

"That said, trifling occurrences and petty annoyances should never be mentioned to your friends."

Cabbie

1856. **ISABELLA** *is sitting by herself in the carriage. She has a piano book on her lap and is practising 'air piano'. She is waiting for* **SAM** *and is agitated that he is late.*

BELLA *(She sees* **SAM** *approaching the cab.)* What took you so long?

SAM *(as he gets into the cab. To* **CABBIE***)* Drive on! *(to* **BELLA***)* Sorry.

BELLA *throws herself at* **SAM***, kissing him passionately.*

(calming her down, overlapping) I hope we're not late for your piano lesson.

BELLA Who cares? I'd rather be here with you. (SAM *is flattered.*) We could talk about furnishings.

SAM *(without enthusiasm)* Furnishings?

BELLA For our home in Pinner. Tell me about it.

SAM Again?

BELLA Please. What have you done since last week? Did you get the table? And the curtains?

SAM Oh, no... I haven't yet –

BELLA What did you decide about the wallpaper?

SAM Nothing. I'll get some samples.

BELLA You said that last week.

SAM What have *you* been doing?

BELLA Oh, you know. Teaching the younger children their French verbs, helping Granny Jerrom make the children some new clothes.

SAM What did you make?

BELLA Four petticoats, two dresses and three shirts.

SAM Lord!

BELLA And all week I've had the strangest notion...

SAM What?

BELLA *(coyly)* Do you really want to know?

SAM Go on...

BELLA I kept thinking what fun it would be to be locked in a cupboard with you.

SAM *(going to kiss her)* You naughty girl!

BELLA *(she quickly breaks away)* Why didn't you come to Epsom last Sunday? *(SAM sits back defensively.)* I looked out for you all afternoon.

SAM I was busy with work.

BELLA My parents think you are avoiding them.

SAM I doubt they care, they hate me!

BELLA They don't hate you.

SAM There was nothing but hate from the first moment they saw me!

BELLA Well, you don't do yourself any favours!

SAM How do you mean?

BELLA Missing dinner engagements! Sending me letters on any old scrap of paper that's lying in the office... you know I cried all Sunday evening when you didn't show...it's as if you don't want to see me!

SAM You know that's not true. Things are just very busy at the moment. Please Bella, try and understand.

BELLA I'll try, but it does seem unfair. We're getting married in two weeks and I barely see you! I hope it will be different when we're married.

SAM Of course it will! *(pause)* You'll be pleased to know there are lots of cupboards in our new home!

He kisses her neck.

BELLA *(dreamily)* To think...in a few short weeks I will become your property.

SAM What?

BELLA I just thought –

SAM I don't want to *own* you, I want to love you! I want us to make our choices together, equally, you and me...

BELLA Really?

SAM There isn't a person whose opinion I value more than yours Bella. Whatever we face, we'll face it together.

BELLA *smiles. The carriage comes to a halt.*

[MUSIC NO. 3b. "TOGETHER"]

Look...when you get back to Epsom, why don't you send me a letter reminding me of all the things I need to do for our house? I want you to be happy there.

He kisses her goodbye.

[MUSIC NO. 4. "I LOVE A LIST"]

BELLA Goodbye.

The carriage disappears. BELLA *is alone at her writing desk.*

As requested, my love, I have made a list of all the things left that we need for our little house together. One bread-grater, one colander, three block-tin saucepans, one large boiling-pot, two sets of skewers, one flour box and three jelly moulds. *(With satisfaction)* Ooo...

I LOVE A LIST.
JOTTING DOWN,
CHECKING THROUGH,
ENSURING NOTHING HAS BEEN MISSED.
I LOVE A LIST.
TOTTING UP,
TICKING OFF,
A LITTLE FLICKING OF THE WRIST!
IT'S A SKILL, IT'S AN ART
IT'S A THRILL, WELL, IT'S A START ...
OOH, I LOVE A LIST!

She returns to her letter.

Now, Sam, I really must insist we have the following: salad forks, fish forks, oyster forks, dinner forks, fruit forks, and of course dessert forks.

OH AND CHEESE FORKS.

SEE, I LOVE A LIST.
NICE AND CLEAR,
NICE AND CLEAN.
AND IT'S THE BEST WAY TO ASSIST!
WHEN YOU'VE A LIST:
'IS IT DONE?'
'LET ME CHECK;'
'NO IT'S NOT.'
YOU SEE? ANYONE CAN GET THE GIST!

HOW ELSE CAN YOU EVER HOPE TO EXECUTE A PLAN?
LEAVE IT UP TO CHANCE?
LEAVE IT TO A MAN?

BETTER MAKE A LIST!
WHAT TO DO,
WHAT TO BUY;
THE THINGS ON WHICH WE WILL SUBSIST!
MAKE A LIST!
A TO Z,
ONE TO TEN,
OFTEN MORE!
I FIND IT TRICKY TO DESIST!

HOW ELSE CAN YOU EVER HOPE TO REALISE A GOAL?
A WOMAN WITH A LIST IS A WOMAN IN CONTROL ...

WE CANNOT WALK THE HALLS OF POWER;
WE CANNOT GOVERN THE LAWS OF MAN;
WE CANNOT SPEAK OF THINGS BEYOND US,
SO A WOMAN DOES WHAT A WOMAN CAN;
WE HAVE TO LOVE, OBEY AND HONOUR;
WE HAVE TO WEATHER EVERY WIND THAT BLOWS;
WE HAVE TO KEEP THINGS TICKING OVER,
AND A WOMAN LIVES BY WHAT A WOMAN KNOWS ...

SO MAKE A LIST!

PLAN IT OUT,

THINK IT THROUGH,

BUT BE PREPARED TO BE DISMISSED ...

'DON'T NEED A LIST!'

YES WE DO, YES WE DO, YES WE DO!

I CLENCH MY HAND INTO A FIST!

HOW ELSE CAN WE EVER HOPE TO ORGANISE OUR LIVES?

I KNOW WE'RE NOT YET MARRIED, SAM,

BUT TILL THAT DAY ARRIVES

WE NEED A LIST!

SO I WILL PERSIST!

DON'T YOU SEE, MY DARLING, THIS IS SIMPLY ONE OF MANY,
    MANY OF THE WAYS WE'RE GOING TO HAVE TO COEXIST?

I LOVE A LIST.

Yours affectionately. B.

I really do...

Marriage

A young, upper-class lady sits at her writing desk.

AMABEL My mother always said that a young lady's main aim in life was to make sure that she was a suitable candidate for marriage. The most desirable of women have a wide range of accomplishments, so it was perfectly logical to me that I should practise the piano, study watercolour and speak four languages – in short, do everything I could to give myself an advantage... I could not have been more prepared.

There I was on my wedding day, triumphant in my achievement, and then it dawned on me, what about the wedding night? I simple hadn't thought beyond the ceremony. Legally I knew that I was now the property of my husband, but what would he actually do with me? I had a *vague* idea from one of the other girls at finishing school, but what if I got it wrong? I was so nervous I could barely eat the charlotte russe. The worst of it was that I could *only* ask my mother and she said, 'It was not a thing she could be expected to speak of...' Naturally that sent me reeling and I remember thinking, Oh God! Is it really that bad?

AMABEL *laughs, remembering.*

Of course, it was all fine in the end. More than fine. You know, it's frowned upon to say that you actually like "it". Any whiff of enjoyment and you're considered a whore. In fact, I remember reading a piece that said, "The majority of women, happily for them, are not very much troubled with sexual feeling of any kind". I wonder how on earth he came to that conclusion?!

[MUSIC NO. 5. "I BELONG TO YOU"]

10th July 1856 SAM *and* BELLA's *wedding night.*

ISABELLA *is alone in the room.* SAM *appears at the door.*

SAM May I come in?

BELLA Yes. I am ready.

SAM Bella...

BELLA Mrs Beeton now, if you please.

SAM Mrs Beeton...

BELLA
    I HAVE YOUR NAME ...

SAM
    A NOBLE START.

BELLA
    I HAVE YOUR WORD AND YOUR BOND
    AND THE WHOLE OF YOUR HEART!
    YET I BELONG,
    I BELONG TO YOU.

BELLA *awkwardly walks away from him and goes to undress.*

SAM What are you doing?

BELLA *(blushing)* I don't know. What should I do?

   SAM *goes towards her reassuringly.*

SAM
   YOU TOOK MY NAME ...

BELLA
   AN ACT OF LOVE,

BOTH
   IN SIGHT OF GOD AND OF MAN
   AND THE STARS UP ABOVE,

SAM
   BUT I BELONG,
   I BELONG TO YOU.

BOTH
   ALL THE VOWS ALL THE LAWS
   ALL MY THOUSANDS OF FAILINGS AND FLAWS
   DON'T MEAN A THING IF YOU ARE MINE
   AND I AM YOURS.

SAM
   YOU HAVE MY NAME ...

BELLA
   SO WE ARE ONE ...

BOTH
   THIS IS THE LIFE THAT WE SHARE
   AND IT'S FINALLY BEGUN

BELLA
   NOW I BELONG TO YOU

SAM
   NOW I BELONG

BOTH
   TO YOU.

1857 August. Office

*The bustle of S.O. Beeton. The office is in a perpetual
state of disarray, papers are haphazardly stacked, the
desk is a mess. There is no order.* SAM *has spent the night
in the office and is doing up his tie when* FRED *walks
in. There is an air of morning ritual in their exchange.*

FRED Good morning Mr. Beeton!

SAM *(light and breezy)* Good morning Mr. Greenwood!

FRED And is it a fine day in the world of publishing?

SAM It is indeed! Productivity is high and costs are average –

FRED And income?

SAM Decidedly low...!

FRED Pity!

SAM Still, today is a new and glorious day where anything could
happen. I have a good feeling, Fred.

FRED Stayed in the office again, did you? Doesn't Isabella mind?

SAM Not at all.

FRED It can't be long now.

SAM What?

FRED The baby.

SAM Oh, that! Any day!

FRED I expect you're worried about the birth –

SAM Certainly not!

FRED Really?

SAM There's nothing to worry about! It's a mere...effort of
nature!

FRED *looks unconvinced.*

Her mother gave birth to seventeen children *and* looked after a further four from her stepfather's first marriage! It's in her blood!

FRED They have twenty one children!

SAM Yeah, they live in the grandstand at Epsom. Bella's stepfather is clerk of the course.

FRED What happened to his first wife?

SAM Erm... I think she died giving birth to their fourth child.

FRED Unlucky.

SAM Yes...now let's stop this chatter and concentrate on what we do best.

FRED *gives him a letter. As soon as* SAM *starts reading, the music begins to play.*

[MUSIC NO. 6a. "LETTER – ON FABRIC"]

FABRIC WOMAN

TO THE ENGLISH-WOMAN'S DOMESTIC MAGAZINE,
FIRSTLY MAY I THANK YOU FOR A STERLING PUBLICATION
YOU GIVE SUCH GUIDANCE TO THE LADIES OF THE NATION!
TRULY...

SAM I like her already!

FABRIC WOMAN

NOW, I HAVE OFTEN THOUGHT THAT THERE IS SOMETHING
    QUITE OBSCENE,
IN LADIES OF AN AGE WHO STILL INSIST ON WEARING SATIN;
ONE SHOULD NOT WEAR A FABRIC THAT ONE COULD NOT
    FIND A HAT IN ...
TRU –

SAM *crumples up the letter.*

SAM Who on earth does she think she is policing others' fashion choices?! Next!

[MUSIC NO. 6b. "LETTER – ON ENTERTAINING"]

ENTERTAINING WOMAN

    HELP.

    I NEED YOUR HELP.

    You see...

    MY HUSBAND IS A MAN OF BUS'NESS

    AND HE'S INVITED CERTAIN CLIENTS TO DINE;

    THERE'S A STRONG POSSIBILITY THEY'RE ALL GOING TO DIE

    IF THEY'RE FORCED TO SWALLOW COOKING LIKE MINE!

    I look forward to a response at your earliest convenience...

FRED We get hundreds wanting advice on cookery –

SAM How dull! *(He screws it up.)* Is there nothing a bit juicier? Maybe an article...

FRED I did come across a new movement to make divorce possible without parliamentary approval –

SAM Fred, as much as I wholeheartedly agree with that sentiment, you must remember we have to avoid at all cost anything that might be considered as "news" and therefore liable to that killer of journalism – the newspaper tax.

FRED Of course...

SAM Only the rich can afford that luxury of keeping the masses informed! (**SAM** *looks through a pile of papers.*) Oooo, now this looks more interesting, yes, how about this?

[MUSIC NO. 6c. "LETTER – ON CORSETRY"]

CORSET MAN

    DEAR MR EDITOR,

    PLEASE, SHARE YOUR THOUGHTS

    ON THE PRACTICE OF LACING THE FEMININE FORM;

    I SPEAK OF CORSETS, OF COURSE!

    I'VE HEARD THAT SOME LADIES RESIST IT,

    THE WHALEBONE IS SAID TO CAUSE PAIN;

    BUT WHAT IS A LITTLE DISCOMFORT,

WHEN YOU THINK OF THE HOURGLASS SHAPE YOU'LL
   ATTAIN?
TIGHTER AND TIGHTER YOU PULL IT,
IGNORING HER AS SHE PROTESTS;
REDUCING THE SIZE OF HER WAISTLINE
AND INCREASING THE CURVE OF HER –

FRED You can't print that! My wife would have a fit! Why?! It creates a genre of its own!

SAM It's a slippery slope to fantasy, fornication and pure filth – the question is would it make money?

The two **MEN** *consider. There is a knock on the door.*

BELLA *enters. Heavily pregnant.*

BELLA Sorry, am I disturbing?

SAM *quickly screws up the letter and throws it behind him.*

SAM Bella my love, what are you doing here?!

BELLA Hello Fred. *(looking around in slight horror at the mess)* This is where you work?

SAM Yes, this is where it all happens! Do you like it?

BELLA Lovely...

She looks around for somewhere to sit.

SAM Let me find you a seat.

SAM *uncovers a seat. She sits down.*

How did you get here?

BELLA By the train.

SAM *and* **FRED** *both stop what they are doing to look at her in horror.*

FRED *(faltering)* The...train?

SAM What were you thinking? It must have been crammed with men going to work at this time of day?

BELLA We were packed in like sardines, I won't lie, I had to fold my dress and show my ankles just to make it as far as Euston.

FRED I really don't think a woman in your condition should be making that kind of journey.

BELLA What else could I do? I've already swept and washed the house more times than I care to remember!

SAM See! She's made of strong stuff is our Bella!

BELLA Please... Don't let me stop you doing your work. I only wanted a change of scenery.

SAM Would you mind? There is rather a lot to do.

BELLA I'll just sit here for a bit.

SAM Here Fred, you read these. (*He passes* FRED *the letters.*) I'll get on with that translation.

[MUSIC NO. 6d. "LETTER – FROM CUPID'S LETTER BAG"]

CUPID'S LETTER BAG WOMAN
DEAR SIR,
PLEASE ADVISE ME;
A FRIEND OF MY HUSBAND'S HAS STARTED MAKING CALLS,
AT TIMES HE KNOWS MY HUSBAND IS AWAY;
AND I REMARK A CERTAIN FREEDOM IN HIS MANNER,
WHICH MERE POLITENESS DOES NOT EVER SEEM TO QUELL.
PRAY SIR,
PLEASE FORGIVE ME,
THIS FRIEND HAS BEEN SO KIND TO US IN MONET'RY AFFAIRS;
I FEAR THAT IT WILL MAKE MY HUSBAND ANGRY,
HE'S ALWAYS BEEN A JEALOUS, BUT AN HONOURABLE MAN.
I'M ANXIOUS NOW TO KNOW WHAT COURSE I SHOULD
    PURSUE.

BELLA *has been listening/reading the letter over* FRED'*s shoulder.*

BELLA Sounds like he needs a kick in the town halls, if you know what I mean!

FRED *is amused.*

FRED I'm not sure we can write that!

SAM *(distracted by their camaraderie)* What's that?

BELLA Nothing.

SAM Look, Bella, your French is better than mine: *jupon* – is that a dress or a skirt?

BELLA It's a petticoat.

SAM Oh...good job I checked. And *engageantes en satin*?

BELLA *Engageantes en satin?* They're false sleeves in satin... *(aside to* FRED*)* ...of course only suitable for younger ladies.

The MEN *look at her.*

SAM Really?

BELLA *(with authority)* I think so. Look, would it help if I did your translation for you?

SAM *(looking at* FRED *they both realise what an asset she could be)* I think that would be remarkably helpful.

BELLA *(she looks at it)* Would you like me to correct the bit you've already done?

SAM *(embarrassed)* Yes, please. Fred, can you move these papers somewhere?

FRED Certainly, I'll put them over there.

FRED *moves the papers to make space for* BELLA.

BELLA How many children do you have now, Fred?

FRED Five.

SAM Your wife must be an expert!

BELLA *(jovially)* Perhaps we could call on her for some tips!

> **SAM** *indicates to* **BELLA** *behind* **FRED***'s back that they shouldn't.*

FRED That's very kind of you...but she's not been very well.

> **SAM** *indicates that she likes a drink.*

BELLA I'm sorry to hear that, please send her our regards.

FRED Thank you. I will.

BELLA I'm just hoping I can get through it with no complications.

FRED I'm sure you will. You're young and strong and have good breeding... *(He smiles.)* Sam, it really is the most wonderful thing to behold!

BELLA *(surprised)* You were there at the births?

[MUSIC NO. 6e. "FRED"]

FRED God no! I meant afterwards! When I held my first child I raised my head to heaven, and I thanked the Lord.

[MUSIC NO. 7. "YOU THERE"]

My little girl looked up at me and I swear she smiled. I promised her there and then that I would never let any harm come to her... I truly cherish that moment.

The scene changes to **BELLA***,* **SARAH** *and* **AMABEL** *with their new-borns, in various nurseries.*

BELLA
> YOU, THERE,
> LOOKING AT ME;
> I SEE YOU!
> ME, HERE,
> LOOKING AT YOU;
> FEET SO SMALL,
> EYES SO UNBEARABLY BLUE!

BELLA

YOU, THERE,
QUIET AT LAST
SLEEP, PLEASE,
SLEEP!
ME, HERE,
HOLDING ON
FAST;
STILL NOT SURE

JUST WHAT I'M
SUPPOSED TO
BE DOING BUT
YOU, THERE!
STEALING MY
HEART!

HALF OF US,
ALL OF YOU,
MINE!
ME, HERE,
BROKEN APART!

WORTH THE
PAIN,
WORTH THE
FEAR,
WORTH ALL THE
WOND'RING
HOW ON EARTH I
WILL COPE NOW
YOU'RE HERE ...

YOU, THERE,
NEARLY ASLEEP;
DON'T MIND ME!

SARAH

YOU THERE!
GOT A SET OF
LUNGS
ON YOU!
PLEASE, SLEEP!
ME, HERE,
HOLDING ON
FAST;
SO MANY OTHER
THINGS I'M
SUPPOSED TO BE
DOING BUT
YOU THERE!
LOOKING AT ME!

ALL OF YOU,
MINE!

ME, HERE,
BROKEN APART!

NEVER GETS
EASIER,
THE WONDERING
HOW WE'LL COPE
NOW YOU'RE
HERE!

AMABEL

ME HERE
HOPING TO
LEARN
SOME OF THE
THINGS THAT I
THINK I SHOULD
BE
DOING BUT

YOU THERE!
HALF OF US,

ALL OF YOU,
MINE!
DOESN'T EVEN
FEEL
LIKE
ME HERE, TORN
APART.

WORTH THE
FEAR
BUT
WORTH ALL THE
EARTH YOU'RE
HERE!

ME, HERE,
SO TIRED I
   COULD WEEP,
BUT EVERY
   THOUGHT,
EV'RY CARE,
EV'RY DREAM,
EV'RY PRAYER
IS FOR YOU
   THERE!
YOU THERE!

[MUSIC NO. 8. "HOW WE RISE"]

A cheeky cockney **BARKER** *appears on stage, introducing us to three "***COUPLES***," one from each echelon of society. One* **MAN** *plays all three husbands, changing his hat or jacket as he moves from* **WOMAN** *to* **WOMAN**. *When the* **BARKER** *speaks as one of the people on display, the* **MAN** *or* **WOMAN** *in question mimes their words like a puppet show. When the actor actually speaks, the character name is given below.*

BARKER

THERE IS A UNIVERSAL TRUTH THAT CAN BE SEEN,
NO MATTER WHERE YOU WORK, OR WHERE YOU SUP.
IF YOU'RE A BARONET OR BARKER, OR SOME BUGGER IN
   BETWEEN,
EV'RYONE WANTS TO MOVE UP!

The **FIRST COUPLE** *are brought into view.*

MEET THE JONESES,
PEGGY AND PETE.
HE'S A COBBLER,
SHE'S A COOK FOR A HOUSE ON HARLEY STREET.
THEIR CHILDREN,
THEY WORK A BIT TOO – DON'T WORRY!
IT'S JUST A BIT O' SHOESHINE,
ISN'T DOWN A COAL MINE!
EV'RYBODY'S GOT TO EARN A BOB OR TWO!

BUT PEGGY DREAMS OF HAVING SERVANTS OF HER OWN,
AND PETE SAYS "BE REALISTIC!", SO SHE TRIES.
"THE BEST THAT WE CAN HOPE IS THAT OUR DAUGHTER
    WHEN SHE'S GROWN,
WILL MARRY SOMEONE JUST A LITTLE BETTER!"

PETE *(offended)* Oh!

BARKER *(as Peggy)* 'That's how we rise!'

'**PETE**' *changes his hat and links arms with the next*
WOMAN.

HERE'S MATILDA,
MYRA FOR SHORT.
HER HUSBAND CHARLIE
IS IN INSURANCE – HE'S A DREARY SORT;
THEIR SERVANTS,
(WELL, THEY'VE ONLY GOT ONE, IT *IS* CLAPHAM!)
SHE PICKS UP ALL THE SHOPPING,
DOES A BIT OF MOPPING,
DOESN'T REALLY CARE IF DINNER'S OVERDONE.

BUT MYRA DREAMS OF HAVING LADIES ROUND FOR TEA,
AND CHARLIE SAYS, "D'YOU REALLY THINK THAT'S WISE?"
SO MYRA SAYS,
"THE BEST THAT WE CAN HOPE, HERE IN THE PETTY
    BOURGEOISIE,
IS MOVING SOMEWHERE JUST A LITTLE BETTER!"

CHARLIE What's wrong with Clapham?

BARKER *(as* **MYRA***)*
"THAT'S HOW WE RISE!"

ALL
TIME WAS
YOU WERE EXPECTED TO JUST STAY WHEREVER DESTINY HAD
    FOUND YOU
TIME WAS

BARKER
YOU WERE A PEASANT OR A SERVANT OR A SOLDIER

+MAN

> AND IT DIDN'T GET MUCH BETTER AND YOU DIED OR YOU
>> GOT OLDER.

ALL

> BUT WHERE LIFE WAS ONCE A JOURNEY
> NOW IT'S MUCH MORE LIKE A LADDER,
> AND IT ISN'T JUST THE FAT CATS CLIMBING UP AND GETTING
>> FATTER,
> NO IT'S EVERYBODY CLIMBING OUT THE DARK AND DIRTY
>> CRAPPER
> TO THE SKIES!
> EYES ON THE PRIZE!

*The final "**COUPLE**" are presented – a swaggering baronet and his mousy wife.*

BARKER

> LORD CADOGAN
> MARRIED SALLY VINE.
> HE WAS A PENNILESS PHILAND'RER,
> BUT HER FATHER MADE A MINT ON THE RAILWAY LINE.
> THEIR FORTUNE,
> CAME MIGHTY QUICK, DIDN'T IT SAL?
> MAKES HER AWFUL NERVOUS,
> ALL THAT SILVER SERVICE,
> SHE'S A LITTLE WORRIED DOUGIE THINKS SHE'S THICK!
>
> SO SALLY DREAMS OF LEARNING ETIQUETTE AND CLASS,
> AND DOUGIE SAYS "I HATE TO CRITICISE,
> BUT THE BEST THAT YOU CAN HOPE WHEN TRYING TO FIT IN
>> WITH THE BRASS IS TO –"

CADOGAN Keep your *fucking mouth shut.

*can be fucking, bloody or wretched depending on the age group!

There is a long, shocked pause.

BARKER *(as* **CADOGAN***, but sweetly)*

THEN THEY MIGHT JUST THINK YOU'RE BETTER ...!

THAT'S HOW WE RISE!
THAT'S HOW WE RISE!
THAT'S HOW WE RISE!

ALL

THAT'S HOW WE RISE!

Working

SARAH I met my husband, Henry, at the local fair. He sat next to me and we got talking, just simple stuff, y' know, about the weather and that, but that was how it started. He made me laugh *so* much and he made me feel *so* comfortable, that before I knew it we were sharing a ham sandwich and a piece of fruitcake that his mam had won first prize for. Of course, he's not like that now.

Poor Henry. After we got married he found it hard to find a job so he had to take anything he could, y'know, farm work and such, but then we heard about the factory work in Manchester. They were offering a better wage for less hours. And regular like. No evenings. Things were changing, you could feel it – cities bursting into life up and down the country. People were making money like never before and we wanted to be part of it, besides, before long we had so many mouths to feed that we had to give it a try, *so*, we packed up everything and took the train.

Beat.

Do you want to know how many children I have? Eight! Blessed. Henry says he can barely count the little buggers. It's a wonder how I did it! Of course, it wasn't all plain sailing, there were a couple that didn't make it, but I don't feel sorry.

[MUSIC NO. 9. "SAMUEL – 25TH AUGUST 1857"]

I could just *tell* that the little one wasn't, y'know, right. You *have* to tell yourself that, but it doesn't make it any easier...

We see **BELLA** *alone in her nursery. It becomes clear that the cot is empty. As she weeps over the death of her firstborn, the* **WOMEN** *of the chorus appear in the shadows and sing wordlessly to her – sharing her grief.*

1858 January. Office – Two

It is a cold day in January. **SAM** *and* **FRED** *are working in the office with scarves and gloves on.*

FRED Sam, this has got to stop!

SAM Just leave it Fred!

FRED You can't carry on like this!

SAM Like what?

FRED Charging these low prices and paying these high printing costs! The figures don't add up...

SAM We want everyone to read it, not just those who can afford it!

FRED I know, but –

SAM And don't you think we should strive for the best quality?

FRED Yes, but you have to be able to pay the bills, Sam!

    BELLA *enters.*

SAM Bella! I thought you were going to stay at home.

    There is an awkward silence.

FRED I was so very sorry to hear about baby Samuel...

BELLA Thanks Fred. These things happen. *(looking between the* **MEN***)* What's the matter with you two?

    Pause.

SAM Fred is annoying me!

FRED He hasn't paid the bills.

FRED *passes a pile of papers to* BELLA.

BELLA I thought business was good.

SAM It is!

BELLA Then why haven't you paid these people?

FRED Tell her Sam!

SAM *(lying)* I haven't had time!

Frustrated, FRED *walks away.*

BELLA Can I help?

SAM I really think you should go home.

BELLA Why? I have nothing to do there.

GEORGE FREEMAN *enters. He is a bullish engraver.*

GEORGE *(curtly)* Sam, Fred. I've come for my money.

SAM Mr Freeman! Of course, we were just saying about that. Weren't we Fred? Bella, please can you get Mr Freeman his money?

BELLA *(taken aback at being thrown in at the deep end, she double-takes)* Yes. I'll be with you in a moment.

GEORGE A *woman* doing your accounts, Sam? Desperate times is it?

SAM Not at all. *(sensing* BELLA*'s disapproval)* How's your new wife, George?

GEORGE Tolerably well I guess. Truth is I don't see her much!

SAM How come?

GEORGE *(he spends his time with prostitutes)* I tend to dine *out* most nights.

SAM *(realising* GEORGE*'s meaning)* Oh! *(loaded)* Dining out!

They laugh. BELLA *scowls at* SAM *and he stops.*

GEORGE Truth is a man's gotta eat *real* food, and if you can't stand to eat at home you eat elsewhere.

FRED My missus can't cook either. Bless her.

GEORGE So what do *you* do?

FRED I just eat it. Managing the house just…isn't her forte.

GEORGE Managing? Don't make me laugh. You make it sound like a job! Tell them that and next they'll be wanting to be paid!

He laughs as **BELLA**, *with pursed lips, hands him the money.*

BELLA Here you are, Mr Freeman.

He suspiciously looks at **BELLA** *and checks she's given him the right amount.*

GEORGE 'Till next time.

FRED Let me see you out.

They leave.

SAM I feel sorry for him!

BELLA I feel sorry for his wife! She's expected to do a *job* with no instruction, and because she's obviously failing miserably he's creeping off to the local tavern and tasting *their* delights… and I *don't* just mean food!

SAM *feigns shock.*

C'mon!

SAM What can I say? Not everyone is like you Bella. Some women don't have the aptitude for running a house.

BELLA And yet they're still *expected* to do it!

SAM All I'm saying is that you can't blame Freeman.

BELLA And all I'm saying is you can't blame his wife for no one teaching her to cook or run a home. It's not her fault!

SAM Perhaps you're right, perhaps she simply doesn't know how, but there's nothing *you* can do about it. Now, I have to get back to work.

SAM *walks away to do work.*

BELLA *(shouting after him)* It's alright for you! You were *taught* to run a printing press, no one *teaches* us how to run a home!

BELLA *hears herself saying the line.*

No one *teaches* us to run a home...

BELLA *suddenly has the idea to write* The Book of Household Management.

[MUSIC NO. 10. "GIVE A GIRL A BOOK"]

BELLA
GIVE A MAN A FISH,
HE'LL EAT IT, AND WHAT THEN?
BUT TEACH A MAN TO BAIT A HOOK AND CAST A LINE,
AND HE WILL NEVER STARVE AGAIN!

GIVE A GIRL A BOOK
TELL HER ALL SHE NEEDS TO KNOW...
IT COULD MAKE A PRETTY PENNY...!

It would be a manual for the inexperienced and a reference book for the more proficient.

GIVE A GIRL A CHANCE,
AS SHE SETS OUT ON HER LIFE.
TEACH HER HOW TO STAND UP TALL AND FIND HER WAY,
TO BE A MOTHER AND A WIFE!
HELP A GIRL TO GROW
INTO WHO SHE WANTS TO BE...
LET THE GIRL BECOME A WOMAN...

WOMEN *(dialogue is spoken over the* **WOMEN***) (quietly)*

WE CANNOT WALK THE HALLS OF POWER,
WE CANNOT GOVERN THE LAWS OF MAN,
WE CANNOT SPEAK OF THINGS BEYOND US,
SO A WOMAN DOES WHAT A WOMAN CAN!

BELLA Sam! I have an idea!

SAM Can it wait?

BELLA It's a *business* idea.

SAM I'm listening...

BELLA I was thinking about Freeman's wife and how we could help her, and I thought we could compile a book of all the things a *new* wife needs to know to run a home.

SAM How do you mean?

BELLA A sort of encyclopaedia of household management! Filled with advice, and recipes and everything a wife needs at her fingertips.

WOMEN
WE HAVE TO LOVE, OBEY AND HONOUR,
WE HAVE TO WEATHER EVERY WIND THAT BLOWS;
WE HAVE TO CLOTHE AND FEED A NATION,

SAM Hasn't it been done before?

BELLA Not to my knowledge, I mean there are recipe books, but they're designed for people who already know how to cook. Our book would be for everyone.

SAM How will you start?

BELLA With a list of course! The only problem is I don't really know many recipes –

SAM I know, we can ask our readers from the magazine for contributions!

WOMEN
AND A WOMAN LIVES BY WHAT A WOMAN KNOWS.

BELLA

SO, GIVE A GIRL A BOOK

                                  SAM

                                  BELLA, DARLING, THIS IS
                                      BRILLIANT!

THAT SHE CAN TURN TO
   EVERY DAY;
TEACH HER HOW TO RAISE A   WITH BITS ON COOKERY
   CHILD OR RUN A HOME,   AND CLOTHES!
                                  YOU CAN TEACH HER HOW
                                      TO RAISE A CHILD OR
                                      RUN A HOME,

TO BE HER BEST IN EV'RY
   WAY!

                                    LIKE YOU, BELLA!

GIVE A GIRL A BOOK,
MAKE IT SIMPLE, MAKE IT
   CLEAR ...
GIVE A GIRL A BOOK,
GIVE HER STRENGTH TO
   PERSEVERE;

BOTH

GIVE HER ALL THE ANSWERS,
WHERE SHE ONLY HAS TO LOOK ...
GIVE A GIRL A BOOK!

SAM What will we call it?

BELLA *Beeton's book of Household Management.*

SAM No!...*Mrs Beeton's Book of Household Management.*

Education

AMABEL I didn't have what you would call a rounded education. *(she laughs)* Actually quite the reverse! I learnt languages, music and art with my mother then my brothers would learn maths and science with a private tutor. I so desperately wanted to learn those subjects as well that I sat outside the window and listened to everything I could. One day I was in the shrubbery taking notes on bisexual and hermaphroditic plants, *(aside: Fascinating!)* ...when, to my surprise, my aunt found me. She could instantly see I was doing something my mother wouldn't approve of and instead of telling on me she gave me some advice. "Learn as much as you want, but always keep it a secret." So I did. And here I am, knowing all these things...and I have no one to share it with.

She smiles.

It's not that I don't love my husband or my children. I *do*! I *know* my duty and I know exactly how to run my house *(referring to* Mrs Beeton's Book of Household Management*)*, but I *also* know I have something else I can offer...

[MUSIC NO. 10b. "INTO THE STREETS"]

...and if I can still fulfil my role as a wife and mother, why should it be *so* wrong for me to use my mind for something else?

BELLA *and* SAM *step out of the office on to the streets of London.*

SAM *is looking over his paper, excited by the potential financial gain of the book.*

SAM I think we'll sell fifty thousand copies in our first year.

BELLA Steady! I've got to write it first.

SAM How long do you think it will take?

BELLA I don't know. I have to test all the recipes first.

SAM All of them?

BELLA Yes! Of course, I won't do Eliza Acton's, or the ones I copy from the recipe books – one assumes they tested their own, but the ones from our readers...well, I have to test them as they simply might not work.

A **PROSTITUTE** *waves at* **SAM**.

PROSTITUTE *(calling)* Do you want a nice bit of crumpet?

BELLA *(playing the innocent)* Why is that lady offering you "crumpet"?

SAM Crumpet? It's a *staple* of the nation! *(nervously)* Come on, let's get home.

BELLA *walks towards the* **PROSTITUTE** *and jokingly gets out a purse.*

What are you doing?

BELLA How much are your crumpets?

SAM *pulls her away.*

SAM Bella... I don't think –

BELLA *(ignoring* **SAM** *and enjoying her joke)* And how do you make them? I make mine like a muffin, only in making the mixture it's more like a batter than dough.

PROSTITUTE Ain't she precious!

SAM *pulls her away.*

SAM *(tactfully)* She doesn't mean an *actual* "crumpet", Bella.

BELLA *(pointedly)* I know!

BELLA *goes to leave but the prostitute retaliates at being made fun of.*

PROSTITUTE I remember how *you* like *your* crumpet, Sam! Butter'd both sides wasn't it?!

BELLA *looks at the* **PROSTITUTE** *and then to* **SAM** *realising they know each other. Her game has backfired on her. She quickly moves away with* **SAM** *close behind.*

SAM Bella! Bella!

SAM *stops her.*

Please! Let me explain...

BELLA You're no better than Freeman!

SAM *(sincerely)* That's not fair, it was a long time before I knew you and nothing more than a dismal fumble upstairs at the Dolphin. I assure you. All men do it.

BELLA I *know* men have prostitutes, I just never thought... *(overwhelmed)* She knew your name...!

BELLA *walks away.*

SAM *(following after her)* Bella!

[MUSIC NO. 10c. "SHE KNEW YOUR NAME"]

Home – Pinner

[MUSIC NO. 11. "WISDOM"]

BELLA *is in her house preparing to start her book. The* **WOMEN** *appear around her.*

WOMEN
STRENGTH AND HONOUR ARE HER CLOTHING
SHE SHALL REJOICE IN THE TIME TO COME
SHE OPENETH HER MOUTH WITH WISDOM
AND IN HER TONGUE IS THE LAW OF KINDNESS
SHE LOOKETH WELL TO THE WAYS OF HER HOUSEHOLD
AND EATETH NOT THE BREAD OF IDLENESS.

[MUSIC NO. 11b. "BELLA READS"]

BELLA *(matter of fact)* Household management!

BELLA *pauses looking for inspiration.*

(less sure) Household management...

Longer pause as if trying to conjure inspiration from the ether.

Household. Management.

BELLA *flicks through a few books. As she reads we hear the text read aloud.*

(looking at the cover) The Vicar of Wakefield.

GOLDSMITH "The modest virgin, the prudent wife and the careful matron, are much more serviceable in life than blustering heroines or virago queens."

BELLA Hm. I suppose so.

She finds another book.

LANFEAR "A sensible woman, to preserve the peace and secure the affections of her husband, will often sacrifice her own inclinations to his."

BELLA *(sarcastic)* Thank you, Elizabeth Lanfear. *(turns page)* Oh, there's more...

LANFEAR "By preserving a forbearing silence on the subject of her wrongs...fulfilling the daily routine of Christian and domestic duties, she will strengthen her own virtues and elevate her own character."

BELLA Mmm? *(She looks for another book)* "The Young Bride's Book", by... *(She looks)* Oh! A man... Arthur Freeling.

FREELING "Gentleness, meekness and patience are woman's peculiar distinctions; an enraged woman is one of the most disgusting sights in nature."

[MUSIC NO. 12. "ALL THINGS TO ALL MEN"]

BELLA *(through gritted teeth)* You're not wrong, Arthur.
SO YOU HAVE TO BE A
WIFE AND A VIRGIN AND A CHILD-BEARING MOTHER,

A COOK AND A CLEANER AND A SAINT AND A LOVER,
THE JEWEL IN THE CROWN AND THE JACK OF ALL TRADE,

+**AMABEL**
THE HOSTESS

+**SARAH**
AND THE SEAMSTRESS

+**MYRA**
AND THE MISTRESS

+**ALICE**
AND THE MAID!

ALL, EXCEPT BELLA
IF WE'VE SAID IT ONCE, WE'VE SAID IT TIME AND AGAIN:
A WOMAN IS ALL THINGS TO ALL MEN.

FREELING "The first dispute in the married life is like the first disruption of a river's bank, the injury may be but small, but is continually increasing until the waters rush out, inundate and devastate the country."

The **WOMEN** *have laid a table and* **MYRA** *and her husband sit down to dinner.* **BELLA** *watches.*

MYRA What do you think?

CHARLIE *tries the dish and squints.*

CHARLIE Did you follow a recipe?

MYRA *(insulted)* Yes, of course.

CHARLIE Maybe you should ask my mother how she makes it?

SARAH
AND YOU'RE S'POSED TO BE A CHEF,

AMABEL
CORDON BLEU!

MYRA
BUT STILL GOOD ENGLISH FARE,

ALICE

MAKE THE TEA,

MYRA

DINNER,

AMABEL

SUPPER,

SARAH

PULL A FEAST FROM THIN AIR,

MYRA, SARAH

IT MUST BE CHEAP AND NUTRITIOUS,

BELLA

A CULINARY FEAT;

ALL

"IMPOSSIBLE" MEANS NOTHING WHEN YOUR HUSBAND HAS
TO EAT!

ALICE

PRESS THE CLOTH,

MYRA

LAY THE TABLE,

SARAH

CLEAR THE POTS AT THE END,

ALL, EXCEPT BELLA

YOU SEE,

+BELLA

A WOMAN IS ALL THINGS TO ALL MEN!

After dinner – **AMABEL**'s house.

AMABEL'S MAID From the Master.

AMABEL (*reading a note from her husband*) Fine dinner! Cook
really is the "Angel in The House", I don't know what we'd
do without her! Who'd have thought to put almonds in
with the salmon. (*Aside: I told her to!*) I'm off to the club,

but don't feel you need to wait up for me. Perhaps you can finish that embroidery for my mother?

AMABEL, AND OTHERS
AND YOU'RE ENCOURAGED TO BE FAIR AND ALLURING,
BUT WITH GOOD CHRISTIAN MORALS; AAAH!

AMABEL *tears up the letter.*
HOWEVER, GIRLS WHO ARE PRETTY SHOULDN'T REST ON
    THEIR LAURELS; NO, NO NO!

AMABEL
LEARN FRENCH AND ITALIAN,

+MYRA
PLAY THE PIANO OR FLUTE;

ALL
ON MATTERS OF IMPORTANCE,

AMABEL
WELL IT'S BEST TO STAY MUTE ...

ALL
OUR COMMANDMENTS NUMBER MANY MORE THAN TEN,
BECAUSE –

SARAH *(shouting off to a gaggle of unseen children)* Arthur, put your brother down, put him down! Eliza, fetch that off the stove, Henry, take that out of your mouth! What have I told you – out!

SARAH'S HUSBAND *passes over a baby.*

(SARAH sniffs, it is unpleasant) Cor blimey Molly, not again? Early shift – dinner on the table at five. *(with a kiss on her cheek)*

ALL
ALL THINGS TO ALL MEN!
AND YOU'RE EXPECTED TO STAY
HOME WITH THE CHILDREN WHILE THE MAN EARNS THE
    MONEY,

HE COMES HOME FROM WORK AND SAYS

SARAH'S HUSBAND What've you been doing all day?

Complete silence, and a temperature drop of about ten degrees.

NOT EVEN FUNNY!

THERE IS SWEAT, THERE IS STRUGGLE EV'RY SECOND BAR NONE!

DIDN'T SOMEONE SAY, "A WOMAN'S WORK IS NEVER DONE?"

IT'S A BIBLE QUOTE, SO CAN I GET AN AMEN? AMEN, AMEN, AMEN!

A WOMAN IS, A WOMAN IS,

A WOMAN IS, A WOMAN IS,

A WOMAN IS, A WOMAN IS,

ALL THINGS TO ALL MEN!

Dinner

A young maid sits in a scullery, and talks directly to the audience.

ALICE Oh Lord! Never has there been such an evening! It started at two in the afternoon when cook was taken ill. "Fetch the pork terrine, Alice," was the last thing I had heard her say before she collapsed head first into the lemon tart! Poor thing! The mistress came running down and saw what a mess there was in the kitchen and immediately called for help from Mr Boatman, the butler. As cook was having the cream wiped from her face the mistress turns to me and says... "Whatever shall I do? I know nothing of cooking, and we have some very important guests tonight!" I don't know what came over me, but I stepped forward and I said, "Don't worry, I'll deal with the dinner" and with that I rolled my sleeves up, put my pinny on and got to work.

ALICE *brings out her copy of* Household Management.

I don't know if the dinner was a success or not, I mean... it tasted alright to me – and I'd followed the recipes to the letter. What I do remember is that despite it being scary, I really quite enjoyed myself. I've never been in charge of anything before, and between you and me I quite liked it.

[MUSIC NO. 13. "KITCHEN TRIALS"]

The following montage takes place over several weeks, so there is a sense of time passing between each recipe. BELLA *is a constant in the kitchen. After the first recipe,* SAM *passes through, handing her each subsequent piece of paper. His dress (jacket on, tie undone, etc.) denotes the time of day. A lighting change should mark the moments that* BELLA *is reading as Mrs Beeton.*

BELLA "For the matter of recipes, I am indebted to many correspondents of the *Englishwoman's Domestic Magazine*, who have obligingly placed at my disposal their formulas for original preparations. Nothing, however, has gone into these pages untried. I trust the result of the four years incessant labour which I have expended will not be altogether unacceptable to my countrywomen."

She moves to her kitchen, picks up a recipe and reads:

"FRICASSEED CALF'S FEET"

CALF'S FEET WOMAN
TAKE A SET OF GOOD FEET;

BELLA Good feet? Are those the front or the back?

CALF'S FEET WOMAN
BOIL;

BELLA Boil? In what? For how long? Water, I suppose...

CALF'S FEET WOMAN
LEAVE A WHILE, BUT KEEP THE LIQUOR,
SLICE, AND BATTER IN NICE HOT LARD.

BELLA
WAIT A MINUTE,
"LEAVE A WHILE"?
AN HOUR? A DAY? A WEEK?!
I WISH YOU WOULD ADOPT A MORE PRECISE TECHNIQUE!

CALF'S FEET WOMAN
ADD VINEGAR!

BELLA *(dousing the entire dish in vinegar)*
IF YOU INSIST!

SAM *(entering)* What's that?

BELLA Dead rats in hot vinegary lard.

SAM What?

BELLA Fricasseed Calf's Feet. Would you like a taste?

SAM No thank you.

BELLA 'If the feet are purchased uncleaned, dip them into warm
    water repeatedly, and *scrape off the hair*, first one foot, and
    then the other, until the skin looks perfectly clean.'

SAM *hands her another recipe, and exits.*

Ah, this one seems a little more detailed…"Snipes"

SNIPES WOMAN
    THESE, LIKE WOODCOCKS, SHOULD BE DRESSED WITHOUT
      BEING DRAWN …

BELLA
    WHATEVER THAT MEANS!

SNIPES WOMAN
    PLUCK, AND WIPE AND TRUSS THEM,
    WITH THE HEAD UNDER THE WING!

                    BELLA
                    PLUCK, AND WIPE AND
                      TRUSS THEM
                    WITH THE HEAD UNDER
                      THE WING!
                    RIGHT!

    TWIST THE LEGS AT THE FIRST JOINT,
                    UGH!
                    BELLA *attempts to*
                    follow each instruction.

    PRESS THE FEET UPON THE
      THIGHS,

                    Oh!
                    Becoming increasingly
                    tangled.

    WRAP YOUR TWINE INTO A
      MESH,
    PASS A SKEWER THROUGH
      THE FLESH,
    AND ROAST!

                    Wait! I think I'm stuck…

BELLA *has somehow tied her own hand to the small bird and is holding a skewer between her teeth.*

A QUARTER HOUR AT MOST.

> *(calling out)* Sam?!

SAM *enters with another recipe –* BELLA *extricates herself from the bird.*

BELLA   "They should be sent to the table very hot and expeditiously, or they will not be worth eating."

SAM   This one's an essay...

TRIPE WOMAN

> ME FATHER WAS THE LOCAL BUTCHER
> LIKE HIS FATHER ALSO WAS BEFORE.
> NOW, THERE'S A CUT OF MEAT SO GOOD TO EAT
> IT REALLY WAS A WONDER THAT WE DIDN'T SELL MORE.
> IT'S VERSATILE YET FRUGAL,
> IT'S SUCCULENT AND RIPE;
> IT'S DISCARDED STOMACH LINING,
> YES! I'M TALKING ABOUT TRIPE.
> YOU CAN HAVE
> BOILED TRIPE, FRIED TRIPE, PICKLED TRIPE, ROAST TRIPE,
> BEEF TRIPE, GOAT TRIPE, HOT TRIPE, COLD TRIPE,
> STEWED TRIPE, STUFFED TRIPE, BATTERED TRIPE, POACHED TRIPE,
> GRILLED TRIPE, FRENCH TRIPE, CURRIED TRIPE, SMOKED TRIPE,
> TRIPE SAUSAGE, TRIPE SOUP, TRIPE PUDDING, TRIPE SAUCE,
> TRIPE WI' BEANS, TRIPE WI' ONIONS, TRIPE WITH SHEEP'S FEET

SAM

> WHY DOES EVERYONE EAT FEET?!

TRIPE WOMAN

> CREAMED TRIPE, BUTTERED TRIPE, PEPPERED TRIPE, M—

BELLA   *(cutting her off)* I mean, that's half the book!

She thinks a moment, and jots down on a notepad.

"Tripe may be dressed in a variety of ways." I think that's quite sufficient.

SAM   Got another one here... Seems simple enough.

He exits, handing her a recipe. **BELLA** *reads.*

HORSERADISH SAUCE WOMAN
    PEGGY TULLIVER'S SIMPLE HORSERADISH SAUCE!

BELLA   Horseradish, mustard, salt and pepper. No measurements though! One tablespoon of everything, I suppose...

She begins spooning ingredients into a bowl.

HORSERADISH SAUCE WOMAN
    IT'S A THIN WHITE ROOT WITH A WIDE GREEN LEAF;
    IT'S AN EXCELLENT ACCOMP'NIMENT TO ROASTED BEEF!
    MIX YOUR RADISH AND YOUR MUSTARD AND YOUR PEPPER
      AND YOUR SALT –

SAM returns. BELLA feeds him a spoon of the mixture and he nearly gags at the excess of mustard.

SAM   Urgh, Bella, too much mustard!

BELLA   *(laughing)*
    SHE DIDN'T PUT THE MEASUREMENTS, IT'S NOT MY FAULT!

SAM   Get me some milk, please!

BELLA   No quantities on some things, no timings on others!

SAM   *(glugging milk with relief)* Oh God!

BELLA   It needs sorting out.
    HOW ELSE CAN WE EVER HOPE TO MAKE SOMETHING
      EDIBLE?
    THE ABSENCE OF A SYSTEM HERE IS REALLY QUITE
      INCREDIBLE!

SAM hands her a letter and exits.

RABBIT STEW MAN *(spoken)* Anthony Pailthorpe, Chef to the Lord Edward Seymour, 12th Duke of Somerset, Bulstrode Park, Buckinghamshire

Madam, the art of cookery is an intricate one, and it is my firm belief that a woman has neither the wit nor the patience for its complexities. However, as a man of the profession it pleases me to send you an excellent receipt for Rabbit Stew, for inclusion in your little book.

BELLA Little book?

RABBIT STEW MAN First, catch your rabbit...

BELLA Oh bugger off!
GIVE A GIRL A CHANCE
AND SHE COULD EQUAL ANY MAN!
BUT NO! YOU LIKE TO TELL US WHAT WE CANNOT DO,
AND NOT DISCOVER WHAT WE CAN!
GIVE A GIRL A BOOK
IT'S JUST A "LITTLE BOOK"

SAM *drifts through, and hands her the last letter.*

SAM
AND IT'LL MAKE A LITTLE FORTUNE ...

He exits.

SYLLABUB WOMAN
MY MOTHER'S SYLLABUB
WAS MY FAVOURITE OF ALL HER SWEETS:
CINNAMON AND BRANDYWINE AND FRESH WHIPPED CREAM!

           BELLA
           CINNAMON, BRANDYWINE,
           AND CREAM!
           AT LAST, A SIMPLE METHOD!
METHOD:
POUR THE CREAM INTO A
    BOWL

TAKE A WHISK AND GIVE A
   FEW STIFF BEATS

                POUR THE CREAM INTO A
                    BOWL
                FEW STIFF BEATS.

ADD THE WINE

                ADD THE WINE

                BELLA *adds wine.*

THE BRANDYWINE

                BRANDYWINE

                BELLA *adds brandy.*

THE SPANISH USE A SHERRY
   WINE

                OH! A SHERRY WINE

                BELLA *adds sherry.*

PERHAPS MADEIRA WINE

                GOOD GRIEF MADEIRA
                    WINE?!

                BELLA *adds Madeira.*

ADD SUGAR AND CINNAMON
   TO TASTE.

BELLA *takes a sip.*

BELLA This is delicious!

*She carries on slurping the huge "cocktail" she's just
made.*

WOMAN Please note that the list of fortified wines are suggested
alternatives, and not to be mixed *together* in the same
preparation.

BELLA Oh. I think it's rather good.

SAM *enters.*

(Theatrically tipsy) "The most essential thing to ensure success is to secure the best ingredients from an honest tradesman."

SAM Bella? Are you all right?

BELLA "These dishes are healthy, nourishing, and pleasant to the taste, and may be eaten with safety by persons of the most delicate constitutions.'

Expectations

MYRA When I was first married I managed fairly well. *(pause)* I *thought* I managed fairly well. I could cook a few simple dishes; sausages...soup *(pause)* but after six months a man needs something more. I couldn't ask Mother, after, well... and it simply wasn't the sort of thing one brought up in polite company. "Excuse me Mrs Wilmington, but how do you braise your cabbage?"

I learnt everything I was expected to learn, but it turned out that my childhood education had been an utter waste of time. Young ladies were "expected" to play the piano, speak French and German and read poetry. Why!? Charlie and I didn't have room for a piano, I had never been abroad to use my languages and no husband wants to sit and listen to a recitation of *Paradise Lost*!

It was all pointless, because from the moment we were married I was *expected* to cook and clean and look after every small detail of the house. "Myra, can you pour the tea? Myra, where's the sugar? Myra, the cake needs cutting. Myra, can you come and be mother?" *(pause)* Mother. *(The word is painful.)* All these expectations to fill!

Wives want their husbands to earn more, husbands want their wives to bear children and create a domestic haven, and as to our families...well, if you don't fulfil these expectations they'll brand you a failure.

Pinner, 1859

BESSIE *and* **ESTHER** *come to visit. They are alone in the room nosing around.*

ESTHER I think it's very nice.

BESSIE Esther, it's horrid! Our big sister hasn't even got a maid. Does that lead to a drawing room?

ESTHER I think it's a cupboard.

BESSIE Why are there so many cupboards in this godforsaken place?!

ESTHER How long do you think we have to stay?

BESSIE We've seen baby Samuel now –

ESTHER Why they had to call him Samuel like the last one… it doesn't seem right –

BESSIE I say we have a quick cup of tea and then be off.

ESTHER All right!

BELLA *comes in with a tray.*

What on earth is that?

BELLA I've been baking.

ESTHER Baking?

BELLA I've been testing a recipe.

BESSIE Whose?

ISABELLA Someone who wrote in to the magazine, but it didn't work out as I expected.

ESTHER What do you mean?

BELLA Well, the recipe said it was a cake.

She removes the cloth.

And mine looks more like a biscuit.

She looks at the biscuit and laughs.

ESTHER You really are the most awful cook, Bella!

BESSIE *(scolding)* Esther!

BELLA She's right, I used to be terrible, but I'm really quite good now. *(building up the courage)* You see, I've been doing a lot of cooking recently because... I'm writing a book.

The two sisters look at her in horror.

ESTHER Writing?

BELLA Yes.

BESSIE He's making you work?!

BELLA No, no! It was *my* idea. It's mainly recipes and such.

> **ESTHER** *gasps.*

What's the matter?

ESTHER He's reduced you to a common labourer!

BELLA Stop being so ridiculous, Esther. I'm a journalist!

> **ESTHER** *cries.*

ESTHER That's even worse!

BESSIE *(to* **ESTHER***)* Be quiet, Esther! *(to* **BELLA***)* And what about baby Samuel?

BELLA What about him?

BESSIE Who will bring him up?

BELLA You can work and have children, Bessie.

BESSIE I've never heard anything so ridiculous in my life! Where is Sam now?

BELLA I don't know. At the office I expect.

BESSIE On a Sunday?! Didn't you go to church this morning?

BELLA We never go to church.

BESSIE Lord above!

BELLA Things have been a little hard recently. He's been busy with his new venture – the *Boy's Own Magazine* and I've been concentrating on the book, and of course preparing for the baby...

BESSIE *(bluntly)* You look terrible.

BELLA Thank you.

ESTHER I think we should go now.

ESTHER gets up to leave.

BESSIE *(unable to stop herself)* He should be heartily ashamed of himself letting you live like this! He'll send you to an early grave, mark my words!

BELLA We are working together! Isn't it right to stand by your husband?

BESSIE That it may be, but is he standing by you? That's what I wanna know?!

[MUSIC NO. 14. "YOU THERE (REPRISE)"]

They leave.

BELLA *talks to the baby.*

BELLA Don't listen to your aunts. They mean well, though they don't show it. Now, where do you think your father's got to? Eh? You mustn't think he doesn't care, he's just got a lot on his plate, and when the book comes out I expect he'll slow down...you'll see...

YOU, THERE
LOOKING AT ME
I SEE YOU!

ME HERE, LOOKING AT YOU
TERRIFIED ...

[MUSIC NO. 15. "OFFICE. 1860"]

The place is chaotic. Letters are overlapping, some being shouted.

WOMAN 1 To the *English Woman's Domestic Magazine*, I was delighted to see that Elizabeth Blackwell has become the first woman to have her name entered on the Medical Register, but must she be an American? When will England catch up?

WOMAN 2 Dear Cupid, please advise! There is a certain young man, a butcher by trade who I wish to court and call my own. Until now we've been very friendly and then last week I saw him go a walking with Susan Price, the dressmaker. /What should I do?

CORSET MAN To whom it may concern, I have long been awaiting a response to my letter concerning corsets...

BELLA comes in with the baby and the finished manuscript.

SAM Is that the finished manuscript?

BELLA Yes.

SAM Wonderful!

FRED Congratulations!

SAM halts the celebrations abruptly by passing BELLA the letters.

SAM You can read these now.

BELLA Do I have to?!

SAM No time to rest, there's also this translation...an article to write on how to dance the polka, and the loyalty lottery prizes to distribute.

BELLA sinks on to a chair.

BELLA Oh!

SAM You also need to finish that review on *The Mill On The Floss*. Is George Elliot a man or woman?

BELLA Only an idiot would believe George Elliot to be a man.

FRED Freeman said he thought the workmanship too good to be that of a lady.

BELLA I rest my case.

SAM Can you finish the review, Bella?

BELLA *(juggling other papers)* Yes, after I've dealt with these letters...

BELLA *pulls herself together and tries valiantly to carry on.*

WOMAN 1 *(letter)* I was so thrilled to see your request for embroidery patterns. I myself have hundreds and have made quite a collection. Most tend to be of a religious design, with some depicting the various saints. Please respond with how many you require.

BELLA *(writing on list)* Respond to Mrs J. Clark requesting four designs...

WOMAN 2 *(next letter – arguing)* We don't want to do embroidery – we want more patterns! My neighbour has been wearing a new dress this week that has made every head turn on our street.

BELLA *(to herself)* Where can we get more patterns?

SAM *(to FRED)* This package needs to go to Cologne, this to Paris –

FRED That will cost a pretty penny!

WOMAN 3 I have noticed that the reign of small bonnets is extinct; that dynasty has been dethroned by much larger-sized ones that somewhat resemble a coal scuttle at the front and a loose crown at the back...please advise!

BELLA Sam, we need more dressmaking patterns –

FRED What about these?

He passes her some papers.

BELLA No...these won't do. Women want the *French* designs in the illustrations. Look...

She shows him a letter.

WOMAN 2 *(shouting)* We want elegance not utility!

The baby starts to cry.

BELLA They want something grander!

SAM A new magazine?

BELLA *(brainstorming)* Something regal...

SAM What would it be called?

BELLA Er...The Queen?

SAM That's a brilliant idea!

BELLA It should be lavishly illustrated with regular sections on what the royals are doing, new fashions, gossip and maybe even...politics!

SAM Sounds radical!

FRED Sounds expensive!

BELLA *sits down, burnt out, head throbbing.*

Are you all right Bella?

BELLA Yes, I'm fine.

SAM Fred, write this down, for immediate release – "The Queen! A new magazine for the modern lady, only sixpence an issue, edited by our own Mrs Isabella Beeton..."

SAM *turns to* **BELLA** *and she faints.*

Bella? *(to* **FRED***)* What happened?

FRED She's fainted!

SAM Why?

FRED Sam! She hasn't stopped!

SAM What do I do?

[MUSIC NO. 16. "THE GRAND TOUR"]

The stage is full of people with luggage, preparing to embark on various journeys. Two **MARRIED COUPLES,** *and a pair of debutante sisters, or perhaps a girl with a chaperone. The following is sung by the chorus with a very particular sense of British disapproval and snobbery.* **SAM** *and* **BELLA** *do not sing, but dash madly from country to country, juggling bags, books and a baby, absorbing the cultures and speaking in the vernacular of each country.*

ALL CHORUS
WE'LL TAKE A LITTLE TRIP TO THE CONTINENT;
A WEEK OR TWO AWAY IS ALWAYS TIME WELL SPENT!
OUR EMPIRE COVERS HALF THE MAP,
AND EUROPE CAN BE SOMETHING OF A TOURIST TRAP,
BUT STILL WE SHOULD POP BY AND SAY 'BONJOUR';

OR GUTEN TAG!
IT'S WITH A BRITISH SENSE OF DUTY WE SET OFF
ON THE GRAND TOUR!

SAM *and* **BELLA** *are packing.*

BELLA This is just what I need!

SAM Our first holiday –. *(referring to packages of books)* And we'll deliver these on our way!

BELLA Do you think we have everything?

SAM *(in pause)* Everything on your list.

BELLA *(in pause)* Then we have everything!

SAM Where first?

BELLA Paris!

As they sing **SAM** *exchanges a pile of books for money –
or does some business!*

FIRST COUPLE

THE FRENCH HAVE ALWAYS BEEN A LITTLE HARD TO BEAR;
NAPOLEON MADE EVERYTHING SO AWKWARD THERE!
AND YES, WE KNOW THE CHEESE IS GOOD,
BUT IT ISN'T DOWN TO LIBERTY OR BROTHERHOOD!
THE COUNTRY SOMEHOW LACKS A REAL ALLURE;

MAN A French word I believe...

WOMAN Very good, dear.

BOTH

STILL, WITH A BRITISH SENSE OF JUDGMENT, WE PRESS ON ...
WITH THE GRAND TOUR!

The **FRENCH SHOP ASSISTANT** *is trying to get the
attention of the* **WOMAN**.

SHOP ASSISTANT C'est de la broderie Anglaise. *(to the* **WOMAN***)*
Would you like to try it on?

WOMAN Oh, no! I never wear anything that's *French*!

BELLA is in her element in a French dress shop.

BELLA Oh Sam, look at this fabric! Isn't it beautiful! And look
at this dress...

SHOP ASSISTANT La hauteur de la mode! *(The height of fashion)*

BELLA *(writing in her notebook)* Large domed skirt, pantalettes
will be essential –

SAM And a large house...

BELLA Sh!

SHOP ASSISTANT La robe est renforcée avec du crin de cheval.
(The dress is reinforced with horsehair)

SAM Did she say reinforced with horsehair?

BELLA I'll take one!

The **SHOP ASSISTANT** *gives the hooped skirt to* **SAM** *who puts it over his shoulder and buckles under the weight.*

SAM *(to the* **SHOP ASSISTANT***)* What's it made of?

SHOP ASSISTANT Steel!

BELLA Next stop, Switzerland!

Switzerland. Gorgeous vistas of snowy Alps abound.

As they pass through Switzerland **SAM** *drops off another bundle of books for money.*

MEN
WE'VE NEVER REALLY TRIED TO UNDERSTAND THE SWISS;
I S'POSE NEUTRALITY IS LOVELY WHEN YOU LIVE LIKE THIS!
BUT REALLY, IT'S AN AWFUL BORE,
JUST PICK A BLOODY SIDE AND FIGHT THE GODDAMN WAR!
BUT NO, YOU WANT TO STAY SAFE AND SECURE ...
Tucked away behind your alps!
SO WITH A BRITISH SENSE OF HONOUR WE PUSH ON,
WITH THE GRAND TOUR.

MAN Where next?

WOMAN Italy!

BELLA Bellissimo! *(Beautiful)*

Next, Italy. **SAM** *and* **BELLA** *are visiting churches in Northern Italy.* **SAM** *has the baby in his arms.*

A sixteenth-century Benedictine church.

SAM Designed by Palladio!

BELLA Let's go in!

They walk in to find the **ENGLISH TOURISTS.**

Beautiful!

TOURISTS Sh!

SAM *(whispering)* Sorry!

BELLA *(reading tour book)* In the Cappella dei Morti is a painting by Tintoretto.

SAM A rich sense of culture...

BELLA *(writing in her notebook)* Art and architecture at its best!

SAM A must for anyone visiting the Continent!

ITALIANS *Un bambino! Bellissimo!*

SAM He hasn't been very well, he has a bit of a cold.

The **ITALIANS** *coo over the baby sympathetically.*

Ah bellino!

Bimbo bello! Che carino!

Ma guarda, sorride!

The **ENGLISH TOURISTS** *are not amused.*

TWO LADIES
THE ITALIANS HAVE A TRULY SPECIAL WAY WITH ART;
THE PAINTING AND THE MUSIC, OH, WHERE DOES ONE START?
BUT MUST THEY ALWAYS TALK SO LOUD?
I CAN BARELY HEAR THE MONTEVERDI THROUGH THIS CROWD;
YOUR PASSION'S FINE, BUT PLEASE, BE MORE DEMURE!

BELLA *I think it's actually Vivaldi...*

WOMAN Shh!

WELL, WITH OUR BRITISH SENSE OF BREEDING, WE MOVE ON ...
WITH THE GRAND TOUR!

The company collect their bags and move to Germany.

ALL
FACT IS, WE OWN
INDIA, AUSTRALIA, GUYANA AND CEYLON
NEW ZEALAND, IRELAND, CANADA, HONDURAS AND
    HONG KONG.
JAMAICA AND BERMUDA AND BARBADOS AND THE REST ...
IT'S NOT A COMPETITION, BUT OUR EMPIRE IS THE BEST.
THERE'S GAMBIA, SOMALIA, SAMOA AND SUDAN,
THERE'S SINGAPORE AND YEMEN AND OF COURSE
    AFGHANISTAN!
WE RUN THE BALLY WORLD, AND SO I THINK WE'RE ALL
    AGREED:
EUROPE IS A CONTINENT WE SIMPLY DO NOT NEED!

*A long, long pause while we all consider the horror which
awaits us.*

Germany – *Christmas.*

Guest house, **GERMAN WOMAN** *welcomes them with
open arms!*

G. WOMAN Fröhliche Weihnachten! *(Merry Christmas)*

BELLA Fröhliche Weihnachten!

G. WOMAN Machen Sie sich bequem! Kann ich Sie ein Glas
Glühwein anbieten? *(Make yourselves at home! Can I offer
you a glass of mulled wine?)*

BELLA Ja Dankeschön.

    BELLA *drinks the mulled wine.*

SAM That smells delicious.

BELLA Try some.

    SAM *takes the cup from* **BELLA** *and drinks it.*

SAM What is it?

BELLA It's an old German recipe of sugar and spices boiled in red wine.

SAM You should put that in the second edition!

BELLA *(writing in her book) For Household Management*, second edition. Mulled wine... One of the many German Christmas traditions we should embrace!

SECOND COUPLE
NOW, GERMANY'S A PLACE ON WHICH WE CAN DEPEND.
AN INTERNATIONAL POWER AND A LIFELONG FRIEND.
OUR MONARCH WED A PRUSSIAN PRINCE,
AND WE'VE BEEN SAYING DOPPELGÄNGER EVER SINCE
A FRIENDSHIP THAT'S SO SPECIAL MUST ENDURE.

ANOTHER MAN I can't see it ever going wrong, can you?

COMPANY (EXCEPT BELLA AND SAM)
AND WITH THAT BRITISH SENSE OF FORESIGHT
WE ARE DONE,
DONE,
WE ARE DONE.
WITH THE GRAND TOUR!

Lecture On Syphilis

DOCTOR Syphilis *(He lets the word ring around the auditorium.)*

This highly contagious, incurable disease differs between the sexes and typically goes through several stages.

Initially the male subject will notice an ulcer forming followed by a fever, rash and potentially a sore throat. These seemingly insignificant signs soon cease, however, when the symptoms return, as they undoubtedly will, they do so with such severity and force that they render the patient powerless, partially blind and plagued by madness.

By contrast the initial symptoms in the female subject often go completely undetected with little evidence of having been ever infected. Typically contracted on her wedding night from her... *(He pauses to think how to put it.)* husbands premarital indiscretions, she will remain contagious for a duration of around five years. After this period any other minor symptoms will gradually fade away.

However, should the subject become pregnant during this time, they will pass this disease to their unborn child resulting in either miscarriage, stillbirth or should the infant live, they will endure a miserable, painful existence consisting of vomiting, diarrhoea and ultimately an unpreventable death.

[MUSIC NO. 17. "WATCH THE LIGHT"]

BELLA *sits alone in a bright sunlit room. It is morning. Perhaps she is holding a toy or a piece of her son's clothing. The light gradually fades over the course of the song, ending in darkness.*

BELLA

THERE IS NOTHING YOU CAN SAY;
WORDS ARE NOT ENOUGH.
EACH PLATITUDE AND PRAYER
IS JUST ANOTHER WASTE OF AIR,
THERE'S NOTHING YOU CAN SAY.

AND THERE'S NOTHING YOU CAN DO
WHEN YOUR WORLD HAS TURNED TO STONE.
EACH SECOND OF EACH DAY
JUST TICKS RELENTLESSLY AWAY;
THERE IS NOTHING YOU CAN DO ...

SO YOU SIT AND WATCH THE LIGHT
FADING INTO GREY.
THERE'S NOTHING YOU CAN DO,
AND NOTHING YOU CAN SAY
AND NO WAY TO GET THROUGH
ANOTHER ENDLESS, EMPTY DAY,
SO YOU JUST SIT AND WATCH THE LIGHT!
WATCH THE LIGHT!
WATCH THE LIGHT!

AND THERE IS NOTHING IN THE WORLD

THAT YOU WOULD NOT GLADLY GIVE.
BUT EACH HEARTBEAT AND EACH BREATH,
BECOMES ANOTHER LITTLE DEATH,
THERE IS NOTHING IN THE WORLD ...

She stops, unable to continue.

[MUSIC NO. 18. "REVIEWS"]

BELLA *sits alone. The music changes and we hear various voices reading reviews of* The Book of Household Management. *As they are read, time shifts in* **BELLA** *and* **SAM**'*s world.* **BELLA** *is a shadow of her former self and the fight has left her.*

CHORUS   *(variously)* "*Mrs Beeton's Book of Household Management* cannot be spoken of too highly. The authoress of the portly book before us, embraces the whole subject of domestic management."

"Beeton and his good wife *(we presume)* work well together as publisher and editress."

"No lady ought to be without it"

"She shows that while luxurious repasts and sumptuous hospitalities rightly belong to the high and wealthy, there is no monopoly of good digestion."

"The labour of four years, she tells us, has been expended on the work, and it can be truly said that nothing useful nor agreeable has been left out."

WOMAN 1
MRS BEETON SAYS THE THINGS A WOMAN NEEDS TO KNOW:

WOMAN 2
SEV'RAL THOUSAND PAGES OF THE FINEST TIPS A WOMAN
    CAN BESTOW!

WOMAN 3
MRS BEETON SAYS SHE'S PUT THESE METHODS TO THE TEST;

MAN

MRS BEETON'S HUSBAND IS A MAN WHO MUST BE WELL AND TRULY BLESSED!

"Each receipt is described in a clear classification and arrangement: first 'Ingredients', with quantities and relative proportions; then the 'Method' of using those materials, and perhaps most importantly, the cost."

ALL WOMEN

MRS BEETON TELLS US HOW TO BALANCE ALL THE BOOKS!
HOW TO BE A LADY WHO IS WISE WITH WHAT SHE BUYS AND WHAT SHE COOKS!
MRS BEETON TEACHES US THE ELEGANCE OF THRIFT;

SAM

FOR THE MODERN WOMAN, MRS BEETON IS THE PERFECT GIFT!

These are wonderful reviews Bella! The book is proving more popular than Mr Dickenss' *Great Expectations*! This is just what we needed!

BELLA *doesn't reply.*

Of course, we can't be complacent. We need to make constant revisions, and with the success of *The Queen* magazine you'll have your hands full. Bella?

BELLA *turns away from him in exhaustion.*

[MUSIC NO. 18b. "TRANSITION INTO BUTCHER'S"]

Butcher's, 1862

MYRA *and a heavily pregnant* BELLA *are standing in a queue at the butcher's.*

MYRA Are you expecting your first?

BELLA No.

MYRA I always wanted children, but things didn't turn out as I expected.

BELLA Having children wasn't as I expected either.

They look at each other.

BUTCHER That's two pork chops for you Mrs Browne and half a tongue and a pound of mince for you Mrs Beeton, and I've put some extra bits in for one of your famous broths.

BELLA That's very kind of you Mr Hughes.

BUTCHER I hope you feel better for it.

BELLA Thank you.

BELLA *leaves and is stopped by* MYRA BROWNE.

MYRA Are you *Isabella* Beeton?

BELLA Yes?

MYRA As in *Mrs* Beeton?

BELLA Yes.

MYRA As in *Mrs Beeton's Book of Household Management*?

BELLA Yes.

MYRA I thought you'd be...older!

BELLA Sorry.

MYRA No! I'm just surprised. I mean, you must be the same age as me.

BELLA *smiles.*

Sorry, my name is Myra, Myra Browne and I live with my husband Charlie just down the road here in Milton Street.

BELLA And I live with my husband Sam in Bloomfield Road.

MYRA So we're practically neighbours?!

BELLA Yes.

MYRA Well I never!

BELLA Perhaps... *(tentatively)* you would like to come around for tea?

MYRA Really? I mean, yes! I'd like that very much.

BELLA When would be convenient?

MYRA To have tea with you – anytime!

[MUSIC NO. 18c. "TRANSITION INTO BELLA'S KITCHEN"]

CHORUS *(variously)*

MRS BEETON SAYS ...

"After luncheon, calls and visits may be made and received. These may be divided under three headings: ceremony, courtesy or friendship."

MRS BEETON SAYS ...

"Occupations of drawing, music or reading should be suspended on the entrance of visitors. If a lady be engaged in light needlework, it is not inconsistent with good breeding to quietly continue it during conversation."

MRS BEETON SAYS...

"A strict account should be kept of all visits and notice how soon your visits are returned. An opinion may thus be formed as to whether your frequent visits are, or are not, desirable..."

Beeton's Home, December 1864. Morning

Two weeks later. MYRA *is having tea at the Beeton's.* BELLA *is sitting at the kitchen table surrounded by papers.* SAM *enters, getting ready to leave for work.*

SAM Ah, Mrs Browne, you're back...again.

MYRA I hope you don't mind, I just thought I'd pop in to say thank you for dinner the other night and to bring some honey for your sore throat...

SAM That's very kind of you.

MYRA Has it got any better?

SAM Not really.

MYRA Well, this might do the trick, and Bella said you had developed a mild fever?

SAM *(embarrassed)* Oh, it's nothing really.

MYRA Well, if there's anything I can do to help.

SAM Thank you. *(changing the subject)* Bella, do you think you'll finish the edits today?

BELLA I'll try.

SAM Bella is writing a dictionary of everyday cooking.

MYRA How...exhausting!

SAM You'll buy it won't you, Mrs Browne?

MYRA Of course!

SAM I must dash, or I'll miss the 10.52 train.

BELLA Good luck at the bank.

MYRA It was nice seeing you again.

SAM Till later!

BELLA Don't be too late!

SAM *leaves.*

MYRA There he goes again! Tell me, is your husband always
   so industrious?

BELLA Always.

MYRA So, you're writing another book?

BELLA I don't expect anyone will read it.

MYRA I'm *sure* they will! After the success of your first book...
   I heard it had sold over two million copies.

BELLA I highly doubt that.

MYRA It's one of the most successful books ever written!

BELLA It's just a cookbook.

MYRA *(horrified by* BELLA*'s dismissive nature)* Just a cookbook?
   Oh Bella, how can you say that when it's so much more..?

   [MUSIC NO. 19. "DON'T YOU SEE?"]

MYRA Imagine...
   SOMEWHERE IN THE WEST COUNTRY
   A MAID SITS IN HER ROOM;

   We see ALICE *in the background.*

   THE HEARTH IS SWEPT,
   THE SILVER SHINING BRIGHT,
   BUT SHE HAS SO MUCH STILL TO DO!

   SHE TURNS THE PAGES OF A BOOK,
   A BOOK SHE SAVED TO BUY!
   SHE READS OF THINGS OF WHICH SHE NEVER KNEW,
   BUT IS DETERMINED NOW TO TRY!

   DON'T YOU SEE?
   SHE THOUGHT THAT THIS WAS ALL THAT SHE COULD BE:
   A GIRL TO SWEEP THE HEARTH AND MAKE THE TEA!
   BUT PERHAPS THE THINGS SHE LEARNS WILL SET HER
       FREE ...?

   AND SOMEWHERE UP NEAR, I DON'T KNOW, MANCHESTER,
   THERE IS A, A TABLE SET FOR TEN;

SARAH *can now be seen, moving about her kitchen.*

BELLA Ten, good grief!

MYRA

A WOMAN WONDERS HOW TO FEED HER CHILDREN
AND THE NEXT DAY TO DO THE SAME AGAIN.

SHE TAKES A COPY OF YOUR BOOK,

Your book, Isabella!

ON WHICH SHE NOW RELIES!
WITHIN THOSE PAGES SHE IS NOT ALONE!
THE MEAT WON'T BURN, THE BREAD WILL RISE!

DON'T YOU SEE?
YOU'RE HELPING HER BE WHO SHE NEEDS TO BE!
NO WOMAN IN THE WORLD WOULD DISAGREE!
AT LEAST THAT'S HOW IT SEEMS TO ME ...!

BELLA *sighs, and looks at* **MYRA** *for a long time.*

Dismissively.

BELLA

IT'S REALLY JUST A BOOK.
A LOT OF RECIPES AND THOUGHTS.
A HELP FOR GIRLS WHO NEVER LEARNED OR DON'T KNOW
      HOW,
A MANUAL OF SORTS!

                              MYRA *Yes!*

BUT STILL IT'S JUST A BOOK;
IT'S NOT A FLAG THAT WE SHOULD FLY!
YES, I WROTE A BOOK.
BUT I'M NOT SURE EVEN WHY ...

MYRA You can't possib—

BELLA *(frustrated)*

NO! SUET PUDDING, ISN'T POWER;
GETTING DINNER ON THE TABLE ISN'T ART!

FANCY CAKES AND FRIED HASH BROWNS DO NOT MEAN
FREEDOM!

MYRA

BUT DON'T YOU SEE?
IT'S A START …

EVEN NOW IN KENSINGTON
THERE SITS A LADY, TWENTY-THREE OR FOUR.

AMABEL, *at her writing desk.*

SHE HASN'T STRUGGLED FOR THE LIFE SHE LIVES,
BUT THAT WON'T STOP HER WANTING MORE.
SHE LAYS A HAND UPON HER BOOK,
YOU SEE, SHE KNOWS IT CAN BE DONE:

BELLA *What?*

TO REACH BEYOND A LIFE OF CHORES AND CHILDREN,
AND PERHAPS, TO *BE* SOMEONE.

DON'T YOU SEE?
YOU'VE PROVED SHE CAN BE WHO SHE WANTS TO BE!
YOU SAY IT'S JUST A BOOK, BUT IT'S A KEY!
AND ALL OF US ARE YEARNING TO BE FREE …!
DON'T YOU SEE?

*There is a bustle of people before a gavel breaks us into
the trial.*

[MUSIC NO. 20. "TRIAL, 1865"]

*The stage is shared between the court room and the
Beeton home.*

JUDGE Case Ward, Lock and Tyler verses Beeton. *(The* **JUDGE**
looks at the papers.) Mmmm… Mr Beeton, …it says here
you owe the plaintiff the sum of twelve hundred pounds.
Is this true?

SAM I lost a lot of money in shares.

JUDGE So you *gambled* all your wealth away?

SAM I wouldn't say gambled...

JUDGE *(firmly)* Either you can, or you can't pay this sum of money?

SAM I can't.

JUDGE Then you are guilty! *(He hits the gavel.)*

> *We switch to:*
> **MYRA**
>> Sam, can you get some hot water? The baby is coming! Sam!
> **SAM**
>> I'll be there in a moment...

In order to avoid bankruptcy you must hereby assign all business assets and workers—

SAM *(shocked)* Fred? No...

JUDGE *(firmly)* Including *Fred Greenwood* to the ownership of Ward, Lock and Tyler. And by the terms set forth in the agreement you must devote all your time to the publishing business of the plaintiffs. No independent work should be published by the defendant without the permission of his employer. Case dismissed.

> **MYRA**
>> *(cradling the baby)* It's a boy!
> **SAM**
>> I need to see her.
> **MYRA**
>> Let her rest.
> **SAM**
>> No, I *need* her advice...
> **MYRA**

Sam, she doesn't want to
see you.

In the case of Freeman verses Beeton. The plaintiff claims
you have withheld payment for his services on *The Queen*
magazine. Is this true?

SAM No, your honour, as I explained to him, I don't own that
paper anymore...*you* assigned it to Ward, Lock and Tyler...!

JUDGE Then you should have given *him* notice of the fact!

SAM But –

JUDGE Guilty!

Change.

SAM
(*calling*) Bella!
MYRA
You can't come upstairs,
Sam.
SAM
Did she do the edits?
MYRA
Yes, she was up half the
night. Now let her recover.
SAM
Why?
MYRA
She's *not* well.
SAM
But I *need* her help.
MYRA
The doctor says she has an
infection. She has to rest!

And I assign the copyright to all Beeton publications to the plaintiff.

SAM What? This is ridiculous!

JUDGE Consequently you are banned from writing anything under your own name –

SAM What about my wife?

JUDGE Wife?

SAM Yes, *Mrs* Beeton...

Silence.

> **MYRA**
>
> *(exhausted)* Oh Sam! I'm sorry. It happened so quickly, there was nothing anyone could do.

The stage becomes a memorial to Mrs Beeton. The **WOMEN** *read it in their kitchens.*

[MUSIC NO. 21. "USQUE AD FINEM"]

SAM Her hand has lost its cunning – the firm true hand that wrote these formulae and penned the information contained within this book. Cold in the silent tomb lie the once nimble fingers, now nerveless; never to do work more in this world. Exquisite palate, unerring judgment, sound common sense – all these had this dear lady who has gone 'ere her youth had scarcely come. But twenty-eight years were all she passed in this world; and since the day she became wedded wife, her chiefest aims were to provide for the comfort and pleasure of those she loved, and to employ her faculties for the benefit of her sisters, Englishwomen generally. Her surpassing affection and devotion led her to find happiness in aiding, with all her heart and soul, the Husband whom she richly blessed and honoured with her abounding love.

Her works speak for themselves; and, although taken from this world in the very height of strength and health, she felt that satisfaction of knowing herself regarded with respect and gratitude. Her labours are ended here; in purer atmosphere she dwells. Her memory, her presence, will inspire her Husband, left alone, to do his duty; in which he will follow the example of his Wife, for her duty no woman has ever better accomplished than the late Isabella Mary Beeton.

Underscore ends and **MYRA** *enters.*

Succession

MYRA After Bella died it was clear that Sam needed help. Within weeks the debt collectors had stripped him of everything he had left, he had lost his friends, his business, his wife and to settle his debts, Sam had been forced to sell the name – *her* name now, not his. 'Mrs Beeton' had become his most valuable asset and the hardest thing for him to let go. But life goes on, Little Mayson was in desperate need of a mother and Sam was in no state to look after a child. Even Charlie could see that, so we took them in. It was a...special kind of arrangement, but it worked very well. I loved that boy as if he were my own. What more could I do?

Few people had read Sam's beautiful tribute to Isabella. In fact, Ward, Lock and Tyler did everything in their power to make people think that Mrs Beeton was alive and well, tirelessly editing and revising recipes for her fellow housewives. What people don't know is that it was *me* who did those revisions. It was *me* who went every day with Sam on the train to the Strand, and over the years it was *me*, Myra Browne, that became the stout, red-faced, middle-aged woman covered in flour and dripping.

As Bella's voice got fainter in each new edition, the *name* "Mrs Beeton" went from strength to strength: a formidable matron, a household name and a cultural icon. Fancy pastries, jellies and soufflés may seem inconsequential and even frivolous, but in this new industrial world forming around us that book gave us the ingredients for control, the method for freedom and a new-found respect that would lead to...well... *(There is a knowing twinkle in her eye.)* who knows where it might lead?

[MUSIC NO. 22. "FINALE - THE DOMESTIC ANTHEM"]

BELLA

WE CANNOT WALK THE HALLS OF POWER;
WE CANNOT GOVERN THE LAWS OF MAN;
WE CANNOT SPEAK OF THINGS BEYOND US,

MYRA AND BELLA

SO A WOMAN DOES WHAT A WOMAN CAN.

WOMEN *(joining one by one)*

WE HAVE TO LOVE, OBEY AND HONOUR;
WE HAVE TO WEATHER EVERY WIND THAT BLOWS;
WE HAVE TO CLOTHE AND FEED A NATION,
AND A WOMAN LIVES BY WHAT A WOMAN KNOWS!

WE ARE AWARE OF WHAT'S EXPECTED,
WE ARE PREPARED FOR ALL THAT LIES IN STORE;
YES, WE ARE MOTHERS, WIVES AND SISTERS,
WE ARE ALL THESE THINGS,
WE ARE ALL THESE THINGS,
WE ARE ALL THESE THINGS,
AND SO MUCH MORE.

THE END

PROPS LIST

Mrs Beeton's Book of Household Management (as many as required)
Commentators megaphone
Parasols for women at Epsom
Race cards
Picnic hamper
Binoculars
Stubbs of betting slips
Piano book
Coachman's whip
Inkwell
Letter to Sam
Stationery
Papers
Letters
Boxes
Files
Crochet baby blanket/baby bundles
Doll
Crib
Purse
Money
Victorian books
Dinner and cutlery for Charlie Browne
Cast-iron pot
Plates of lard
Recipe cards
Calf's feet
Vinegar bottle
Skewer
String
Snipes
Bowl and tablespoon
Horseradish
Mustard

Pepper
Salt
Milk
Brandy
Madeira
Sherry
Wine
Tea Set for three
Cake and cloth
Finished manuscript
Victorian pram
Packages of books
Broderie anglaise slip
Suitcase
Notebook
Fabric
Mulled wine/cups
Isabella's notebook
Doctors bag
Packages of meat ×3
Tea Set for two
Honey
Gavel
Eulogy letter

ABOUT THE AUTHOR

Helen Watts

Helen trained at Italia Conti on the BA Acting (Hons) course.

After a few years of working as an actress Helen moved to writing and directing, with a particular interest in 19th century classic literature. Adaptations for stage include *Persuasion, Far From The Madding Crowd, Northanger Abbey, Under The Greenwood Tree, Frankenstein: The Year Without A Summer* and *A Christmas Carol.* Book-writing commissions include *Lysistrata* (Royal Central School of Speech and Drama); *The Legend Of Sleepy Hollow* (National Youth Music Theatre) and *Mrs Beeton Says...* (Bristol Old Vic Theatre School). Directing credits include *Persuasion, Daisy Pulls It Off* and *Mary Shelley* (Arts University Bournemouth); *Così Fan Tutte* and *Stone Cold Murder* (Dorset Corset Theatre Company) and *Love is Not A Science* (Royal Central School of Speech and Drama).

Helen is Artistic Director of Dorset Corset Theatre Company and lives in the West Country with her family.

ABOUT THE COMPOSER AND LYRICIST

Eamonn O'Dwyer

Eamonn is an Associate of the Royal Academy of Music and has worked as a musician, composer and sound designer in theatres all over the world. He has written original music for *Mrs Beeton Says...* (Bristol Old Vic Theatre School); *The Legend Of Sleepy Hollow* (NYMT, The Other Palace); *The Comedy of Errors* and *Julius Caesar Re-imagined* (RSC, Swan); *Flesh & Bone* (National Theatre Studio); *Grimm Tales* and *Peter Pan* (Chichester Festival Theatre); *Improbable Fiction* (Mill at Sonning). He is a frequent musical collaborator at the Rose Theatre in Kingston, where he has written original songs and scores for *Hansel & Gretel, Alice in Winterland, The Wind in the Willows, The Lion, The Witch & The Wardrobe, A Christmas Carol, Hamlet, Tess of the d'Urbervilles* and *Arabian Nights*. The score for his original musical, *The House of Mirrors & Hearts,* won the *MTM* Award for Best New Score at the Edinburgh Festival in 2010. After its critically acclaimed run at the Arcola Theatre in 2015 it has now been performed in Australia and the US.

Other plays by **HELEN WATTS & EAMONN O'DWYER**
published and licensed by Concord Theatricals

The Legend of Sleepy Hollow

FIND PERFECT PLAYS TO PERFORM AT
www.concordtheatricals.co.uk